CHILDREN'S
LITERATURE
THROUGH
STORYTELLING

CHILDREN'S LITERATURE THROUGH STORYTELLING

JOSEPH ANTHONY WAGNER
California State College, Long Beach

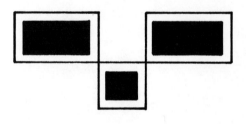

WM. C. BROWN COMPANY PUBLISHERS
Dubuque, Iowa

Third Printing, 1972

Printed in the United States of America

Preface

Children's Literature Through Storytelling is a timely, much needed book in the area of speech instruction. This material has been prepared to assist teachers and all others who work with youth, to tell stories more effectively. No effort has been spared to implement precept with example. The helpful suggestions related to the search for suitable material, its preparation, its presentation, and finally, to the follow-up after a story will make this book a "must" in every instructor's library.

This first edition contains sections on the origin and dissemination of stories. It also provides an overview of the types of literature which will make story selection more meaningful. Of special interest to classroom teachers and recreational workers is the section on dramatic play. Pantomime and role playing are treated separately and a wealth of exercises are included for each.

Children's Literature Through Storytelling will also meet a long-felt need of many parents. Some adults have wished to tell stories to their children but they have been reluctant to try. This book will help beginning storytellers answer such questions as, "Where can I find good stories?"; "How will I know if a story is appropriate to my child's age group?"; "How can I prevent forgetting a story?"; "When and how should I show pictures?". The following pages answer these and other questions for those who choose to introduce children to good literature through storytelling.

J.A.W.

Contents

1

Storytelling:
An Art of Antiquity

THE ORIGIN OF STORIES

The earliest storytellers were nameless primitives who, upon surviving some experience, would recount it to members of their group. Their purpose may have been to glorify their own prowess, warn their companions, instruct, or merely to amuse. These stories were told and retold many times and in this process change occurred. Some details that seemed unimportant were dropped and only subjects of universal appeal survived. Emerging, perhaps after centuries, was a folktale of classic literary form. William and Jacob Grimm supported this theory relating to the growth of stories. They contended that today's tales which have survived the past began in crude, fanciful form, were perpetuated by the peasantry and finally became epics in the hands of literary individuals. Stories told in firelit caves, for example, may have served as the core for an Homeric epic or an experience of Beowulf.

In addition to the simple recounting and refinement of an experience, the origin of stories is also attributed to mans' interpretation of natural phenomena. This belief which is known as the Sun-Myth position, was supported by Max Muller, Eduard Georg Seler and others. This group held that heroes of folk tales are regarded as allegorical representations of the sun, rain, storms, etc. In the beginning, man allegedly had difficulty distinguishing between nature and his own personality. Fanciful interpretations were given to the coming of dawn, dusk, day and night. The weather experienced by the storyteller seemed to influence his attitude. Norse stories seemed more stark, severe and violent than those found in soft, tropical climes. Early man sought to explain the activities of a volcano by making it a god and offering it sacrifices. The movement of fire made it seem alive to primitives. The sun, for example, was believed to love the dew but in a rage, slew her with his arrows. Early storytellers also held that heaven and earth were married and used to be close together until they were separated by their children who had become cramped trying to live between them. Even a simple child's poem such as "The Song of Six-Pence" is said to have symbolic significance; the pie being the earth and sky, the birds the twenty-four hours, the king the sun, the queen the moon, and the opening of the pie, daybreak.

A third group of folklorists believe that all stories began in India and that they may be traced through language to a common Aryan heritage. Joseph Jacobs estimated that at least one-third of all stories common to European children came from India. The close relationship between man and beast which was fostered by belief in animism and transmigration of souls provided fertile ground for the origin of fanciful stories. Additionally, this theory is supported by the presence of Hindus in ancient times who were sufficiently educated and possessed the intellectual ability to conceive and develop plots.

Another group attempted to explain the origin of stories by attributing them to a primitive form of cosmology. These folklorists felt that early man was concerned about his personal origin, how the world was made and why one season followed another. This belief that man has always had a thirst for knowledge, has always been concerned about causality, is supported by the discovery of stories throughout the world that end with such statements as, "And that is why a bear's tail is short." or, "And that is why a robin's breast is red."

What conclusions may be drawn from these various theories? Although there is a basis for each, they in turn may be discounted. Sun-Myth followers run the risk of false analogies and inconsistencies in stories originating in various countries. A large number of these cosmic stories held that the sky was a male and the earth a female. However, a lack of consistency appears in Egyptian stories in which the sky deity is a female. Scholars who believed that all stories began in India have discovered a rival group which contends that the Euphrates Valley is the birthplace of most folktales. Their position is further weakened by the appearance of similar tales in non-Aryan countries. Those who support the cosmologist approach must admit that some primitive tribes are not concerned about their origin and have not even troubled themselves to formulate a mankind creation myth. It would appear that some folklore researchers have had a tendency to impose their own story interpretations independently of those of native storytellers. The idea that an educated researcher is better able to interpret the allegories of primitive people does not carry much weight. It should be the responsibility of a folklorist to objectively ascertain what a tale means to a native raconteur and to his people in terms of their own daily living, religious habits and customs. A psychoanalyst, for example, should not impose alien Freudian interpretations upon a symbolism that a tribe has repeated and accepted beyond the memory of its oldest members. Cosmologists, for example, might do well to learn those factors which motivate a tribe individually and collectively, and not assume that it is necessarily moved by the same stimuli that motivates other groups. As far as the foregoing theories relating to the origin of stories are concerned, each has contributed in varying degree to our wellspring of knowledge regarding orally transmitted tales.

THE DISSEMINATION OF STORIES

Estimates on the number of variations of the Cinderella story extant today vary from 345 to nearly 900. What is believed to be the first Cinderella story concerns an Egyptian maiden, Rhodopis, who was bathing in the Nile. An eagle swooped down, picked up one of her gilded sandals, and dropped it in the lap of the King who was in the act of administering justice in the city of Memphis. Unlike later versions which had a prince or a king fall in love with the girl, this first version had the King become so impressed with the *sandal* that he would marry none but the owner of it. The usual search for a girl who could wear such a small sandal ensued until finally the King learned that a lovely girl visited the Sphinx each day at daybreak. The King and his entourage journeyed to this point, met the shy and startled Rhodopis, matched his sandal with the one the girl possessed, and not long after a marriage took place. Allegedly, Queen Rhodopis and the King lived happily ever after.

Stories of this kind may have been disseminated by many means. Communication between savage tribes may have begun the process. Warfare with its subsequent seizing of women may have furthered the process. Slaves from Africa probably brought stories to the western world. Phoenicians and Viking sailors may have exchanged tales with strangers; the Crusades mingled Moorish and Christian cultures, and the migrations of people from the Orient over the Aleutian land chain to North America could have facilitated story dissemination. Additionally, travelling bards and minstrels who sang and told stories for food and a night's lodging literally carried tales. Once a story became popular, nothing seemed able to contain it. The idea of a one-eyed giant, for example, is found in Greece, Persia, Arabia, Lapland and among the Alaskan Eskimos. Slaves brought to America are believed to have learned tales from the Indians which later became the Uncle Remus stories. Where the Indians learned their versions is problematical. However, one of the slaves' favorite stories, the "Tar Baby," is said to be found in the Ceylonese *Jataka Tales*. Keightley[1] has found equally wide geographic distribution of other famous stories. For example, the *Jack the Giant-*

Killer theme is found in Grimm's "The Brave Tailor" and in "Thor's Journey to Utgard" which may be found in the Scandinavian *Edda*. This theme is also present in "The Goat and the Lion" from the Panchatantra. He has also shown relationship in theme in Grimm's "The Fisherman and His Wife" to the *Pentamerone* tale, "Peruonto," to the Russian story, "Emelyan the Fool," and to the Esthonian tale by Laboulaye, "The Fairy Craw-Fish." This backward glance at story dissemination suggests the vital nature of the communicative role played by storytellers over thousands of years.

Summary

This chapter has listed only four of many possible sources of stories, i.e., stories resulting from man's experience, his interpretation of natural phenomena, the belief that all stories have a common Aryan heritage, and finally, the theory that primitive man was consumed with curiosity to know who he was, how he was created, how the earth was created, etc., and he told stories to satisfy this urge to understand. It is evident from this chapter that once a good story was told, its dissemination occurred in spite of geographic and language barriers. While the study of the origin and spread of stories is fascinating, the important thing for today's generation is the fact that these excellent stories have survived countless years and only await the release of their magic influence by those who are willing to share them orally with others.

---

1. Thomas Keightly, *Tales and Popular Fictions*, (London: Whittaker & Company, 1834), pp.34 ff.

2

Types of Stories

Literature for today's child includes a vast array of stories written in language that he can understand. It ranges in scope from factual discourses on vocational guidance to suggestions for travel to outer space. Wedged in between may be found the great classics of yesteryear and in addition, there are excellent, beautifully illustrated books on nature, fascinating fiction, and highly educational, biographical profiles. The latter, in the hands of competent storytellers, have added spice to most instructional subjects. In an effort to facilitate a choice of stories for telling, material will be considered in four categories: *folk literature* which includes myths, sagas, and folk tales; *narrative poetry* which is divided into epics, ballads and story poems; *realistic stories;* and finally, a discussion of *biographical material.*

FOLK LITERATURE

Myths

A myth is a traditional or legendary story which is concerned with gods and supernatural beings. It frequently attempts to explain some basic truth. These stories are imaginative precursors to scientific research. Commenting on the use of myths Herzberg writes:

> Poets and storytellers of all nations use myths for many purposes. They retell them in their own language—in prose and verse, in short story and epic and play. Dante had Ulysses, the Greek hero, tell part of his story in the *Inferno*. Shakespeare reworks certain episodes of the Trojan War in *Troilus and Cressida*. Goethe tells the story of *Iphigenia* in *Tauris* and Racine that of *Andromache*. William Morris recounts in a long poem the the adventures of Jason in search of the Golden Fleece, and several novels have been written about Helen of Troy and about the adventures of King Arthur's knights.[1]

An understanding of mythology will make literature more meaningful and enjoyable to children. Occasionally one hears reference to "opening Pandora's box" but relatively few persons understand this allusion. The following myth would take but a few minutes to tell and Pandora would no longer be a mystery:

> So men prospered. And as they prospered Jupiter was more and more displeased. He finally settled on a cunning strategem to overcome Prometheus. With the help of his son Vulcan (Greek: Hephaestus), lord of the forge, and of the other gods, he devised a most beautiful woman, named Pandora (a word in Greek that means "all gifts"). Upon her each of the deities bestowed some grace or beauty. Her he sent to Prometheus, and with her went a great jar, such as men use for storing oil; and the jar was carefully sealed. Prometheus, suspecting a trick on the part of Jupiter, refused to accept either the woman or the jar; and Jupiter sent her to Epimetheus, who had been warned by his brother against the wiles of Jupiter. Epimetheus, however, won by the beauty of Pandora, accepted her as his wife.
> "This is my dowry," she explained when Epimetheus inquired what was in the jar; and together they broke the seal and opened it. Immediately a cloud of evils flew forth—all the diseases and troubles and worries that still afflict mankind. Too late, they tried to put the lid back again. But only one spirit remained in the jar: Hope.[2]

Consistent with the definition of a myth set forth earlier, the basic problem or truth this myth explains is why there is so much trouble in the world.

Sagas

A saga is a prose narrative of the heroic exploits of an individual or of a family. Sagas are written to commemorate some factual matter such as war, heroism during natural disaster, or some other outstanding occurrence. It is of significance, for a later consideration of the characteristics of folktales, that sagas glorify the hero-leader cult in a group. Only persons of good lineage who distinguished themselves, could qualify for literary immortality in a saga. The *Volsung Saga* and those commemorating exploits of the Trojan War are typical of this literary form.

Folktales

Folktales may be defined as stories of anonymous origin which form a part of the oral tradition of a tribe or people. In contrast to the saga, these tales are the product of peasants and they extol the virtues of the lowly, the ones considered least likely to succeed by their families or their townspeople. In "The Bremen Town Musicians" for example, the rejected animals prove their worth by defeating the robbers. In "Boots and His Brothers," it is Boots, the youngest and the least promising of the brothers who manages to chop down the King's tree and win his daughter and half of the kingdom. These tales possess a rather persistent moral character. The deserving individual or creature, be it Snow White, Cinderella or the Little Red Hen ultimately is rewarded. These tales usually reflect the dreams and unfulfilled wishes of the luckless and downtrodden. Through folktales, those in authority were challenged and made to look foolish. A classic case in point is the emperor and his advisors in "The Emperor's New Clothes." The recipient of the ridicule could be a king or a husband as in the case of the humorous Norse tale, "The Husband Who Was to Mind the House." Stories of this type apparently were told to amuse or instruct and made no effort to record historical matters. Fairy stories, both ancient and modern, are usually included within the larger category of folktales even though the authorship of modern fairy stories is known.

NARRATIVE POETRY

Although material of this nature may be read more often than it is told, it should be included in the process of sharing good literature with children. At the beginning of the educational program, children need to be led to the discovery of the beauty contained in poetic lines. This should be achieved not through painstaking scansion but through *enjoyment* of meter, message and sound. Narrative poetry should possess such elements of verse form as imaginative language, movement, rhythm, rhyme schemes, symbolism and appropriate word choice. In a few lines, a good poet can express an idea that might require a page or two to develop in prose. In contrast to lyric poems that simply express an intimate feeling of love, depression, or joy, narrative poetry must possess characters and a plot that moves to a climax through a conflict situation. These are general differences between lyric and narrative poetry although each may contain characteristics of the other. Common examples of narrative poetry are epics, ballads, story poems, and nursery rhymes.

Epics

An epic is a long, poetic composition, usually centered upon a hero, in which a series of great achievements or events are narrated in an elevated style. The *Iliad* and *Odyssey*, *Beowulf*, the Spanish *El Cid*, France's *Song of Roland* and Milton's *Paradise Lost* are classical examples of the epic form. The length of these works and the difficulty of the language should discourage a teacher from attempting to read them to her children. However, there are stories within the longer selections such as Ulysses' adventures and Beowulf's underwater battles with Grendel that will hold the interest of upper grade youngsters.

Ballads

Ballads are characterized by rhyme, rhythm and a plot. The story frequently involves tragic, frustrated young love that finds fulfillment after death. They are one of the oldest poetic forms known to the human family and they have survived through the oral tradition. Ballads were told before peasant's hearths and they were also sung by bards in the presence of royalty. They perpetuate the memory of lost causes and lost loves from the West Indies to the range of the American cowboy. Most junior high and senior high school students encounter "Robin Hood and Little John" or Coleridge's "The Rime of the Ancient Mariner." Few of them know that Sir Walter Scott preserved many old tales in verse in his *Minstrelsy of the Scottish Border*. The majority of ballads sung by American colonists were brought here from their native land. "Young Charlotte" is found in the balladry of northern Europe, in Georgia and among Appalachian Mountain dwellers. It is still entertaining folk-song and folktale enthusiasts. Following are selected portions that capture the theme and conclusion of this selection:

1. Now Charlotte lived on the mountain side
       In a bleak and dreary spot;
   There was no house for miles around
       Except her father's cot.

5. How brightly beamed her laughing eye,
       As a well-known voice was heard;
   And driving up to the cottage door
       Her lover's sleigh appeared.

6. "O daughter dear," her mother cried,
       "This blanket 'round you fold'
   It is a dreadful night tonight.
       You'll catch your death of cold."

7. "O nay, O nay!" young Charlotte cried,
       And she laughed like a gypsy queen;
   "To ride in blankets muffled up,
       I never would be seen."

11. "Such a dreadful night I never saw.
        The reins I scarce can hold."
    Fair Charlotte shivering faintly said,
        "I am exceeding cold."

13. Said Charles, "How fast the shivering ice
        Is gathering on my brow."
    And Charlotte still more faintly said,
        "I'm growing warmer now."

17. He took her hand in his—O God!
    'Twas cold and hard as stone.
    He tore the mantle from her face,
    Cold stars upon it shone.

18. Then quickly to the glowing hall
    Her lifeless form he bore;
    Fair Charlotte's eyes were closed in death,
    Her voice was heard no more.

22. Her parents mourned for many a year,
    And Charles wept in the gloom.
    Till at last her lover died of grief,
    And they both lie in one tomb.

The foregoing is a typical example of the ballad and such a tragic theme has been repeated with slight change in both ancient and modern versions of this poetic form.

Story Poems

Story poems frequently contain dramatic, lyrical qualities. Whereas epics extol the virtues of a heroic person or family and ballads typically are characterized by tragedy, story poems may deal with any topic such as dogs, lovers, war, children or any other subject that makes up the mosaic of life. Robert Browning has contributed richly to the human family's treasury of story poems. The following, "Incident of the French Camp" is typical:

You know, we French stormed Ratisbon: a mile or so away
On a little mound, Napoleon stood on our storming-day;
With neck out-thrust, you fancy how, legs wide, arms locked behind,
As if to balance the prone brow oppressive with its mind.

Just as perhaps he mused, "My plans that soar, to earth may fall,
Let once my army-leader Lannes waver at yonder wall—"
Out 'twix the battery-smokes there flew a rider, bound on bound
Full galloping; nor bridle drew until he reached the mound.

Then off there flung in smiling joy, and held himself erect
By just his horse's mane, a boy: you hardly could suspect—
(So tight he kept his lips compressed, scarce any blood came through)
You looked twice ere you saw his breast was all but shot in two.

"Well," cried he, "Emperor, by God's grace we've got you Ratisbon!
The Marshal's in the market-place, and you'll be there anon
To see your flag—bird flap his vans where I, to heart's desire,
Perched him!" The chief's eye flashed; his plans soared up again like fire.

The chief's eye flashed; but presently softened itself, as sheathes
A film the mother-eagle's eye when her bruised eaglet breathes;
"You're wounded!" "Nay," the soldiers pride touched to the quick, he said:
"I'm killed, Sire!" And his chief beside, smiling the boy fell dead.

Alfred Noyes' "The Admiral's Ghost," "The Highwayman," Browning's "How They Brought the Good News from Ghent to Aix," and his "The Pied Piper of Hamelin," are additional examples of the story poems.

Nursery Rhymes

Nursery rhymes tell a story which is limited in content. A child's first exposure to literature is probably through Mother Goose rhymes. The sooner in life this occurs, the better. The progression of literary appreciation begins with hearing poetry and culminates with reading it orally later in life. One of the first characteristics of a nursery rhyme that attracts a child is its rhythm:

> Hippety hop to the barber shop,
>   To get a stick of candy,
> One for you and one for me
>   And one for Sister Mandy
>
>   (Mother Goose)

The child who skips mentally to this shopping adventure will be delighted by the surprise found in the answer to the following:

> Thirty white horses upon a red hill,
>   Now they tramp, now they champ,
> Now they stand still.   (Teeth and Gums)
>   (Mother Goose)

Humor as well as surprise may characterize nursery rhymes:

> The man in the wilderness asked me,
>   How many strawberries grew in the sea.
> I answered him, as I thought good,
>   As many red herrings grew in the wood.
>   (Mother Goose)

> Doctor Foster went to Gloucester
>   In a shower of rain;
> He stepped in a puddle, up to his middle,
>   And never went there again.
>   (Mother Goose)

Nursery rhymes also provide parent and teacher with an opportunity to stimulate young imaginations. In "The Land of Story Books" Robert Louis Stevenson not only includes a guarded indictment of parental play activity but also an invitation to turn a living room into a wild animal safari:

At evening when the lamp is lit,
Around the fire my parents sit;
They sit at home and talk and sing,
And do not play at anything.

Now with my little gun, I crawl
All in the dark along the wall,
And follow round the forest track
Away behind the sofa back.

There, in the night, where none can spy,
All in my hunter's camp I lie,
And play at books that I have read
Till it is time to go to bed.

These are the hills, these are the woods,
These are the starry solitudes;
And there the river by whose brink
The roaring lions come to drink.

I see the others far away
As if in firelit camp they lay,
And I, like to an Indian scout,
Around their party prowled about.

So, when my nurse comes in for me,
Home I return across the sea,
And go to bed with backward looks
At my dear Land of Storybooks.

Another characteristic of nursery rhymes is sheer nonsense which may bring so much joy to young hearts. Nonsense verse does not demand much child-meditation to interpret the message . . . it is instantly understood:

Rub-adub dub,
Three men in a tub,
And who do you think they be?
The butcher, the baker,
The candlestick-maker;
Turn 'em out, knaves all three!
(Mother Goose)

Little children live in a land of giants . . . their elders. In contrast to this environment, nursery rhymes introduce them to many children about their age who have experiences that they can understand. The rhythm, surprise, humor, nonsense and good story book friends of the nursery rhyme period may endear children to literature of this type and enable them to enjoy it even after reaching a more sophisticated age of literary appreciation.

REALISTIC STORIES

Realism is not a definite form in fiction, rather it is an objective, an endeavor to represent life honestly. Literature is said to be a mirror of life with all its beauty and bestiality. Realistic stories seek to represent it as it is. The desire to create realistic stories has been with mankind for centuries. "The Little Red Hen," "Hans in Luck," and "Why the Sea is Salt" are tales that reflect this desire. Hans Christian Andersen's frustrations with society are found in "The Ugly Duckling" and "The Steadfast Tin Soldier." Charles Dickens' *Oliver Twist* and Tolstoi's "The Death of Ivan Ilyich" illustrate the tragedy of the poor and unfortunate. In the United States, Mark Twain accurately depicted river town life through the adventures of Huck Finn; Bret Harte acquainted readers with mining camp life in "The Outcasts of Poker Flat" and Jack London pitted man and beast against nature in *The Call of the Wild.* John Steinbeck captured the poverty and humiliation of economic depression in *The Grapes of Wrath* and in more recent times, Louis Lomax' writing has brought ghetto existence into sharp focus.

Like story poems, realistic stories claim a vast range of interests. Animal stories, sports, life with one's family, sea adventure and excursions into outer space all fall within its purview. Realistic stories may help both parents and teachers develop tolerance in their children. Alberta Armer's *Trouble-maker,* for example, explains the plight of a twelve-year-old whose father is incarcerated and his mother is mentally disturbed. Mimi Brodsky's *The House at 12 Rose Street* develops a sense of appreciation for the trials faced by black Americans in white neighborhoods. *The Hundred Dresses* by Eleanor Estes reveals the savagery of insensitive classmates toward a virtually penniless immigrant girl who lacks proper clothing. This hostility breaks the spirit of the family and they decide to leave the neighborhood.

Literally thousands of stories with a realistic impact await storytellers who possess the energy and patience to match appropriate stories to the needs of their audience.

BIOGRAPHICAL STORIES

This form of literature is enjoying a great period of popularity. The flood of biographical books published in this century prompts a reader to wonder why material of this type enjoys such demand. The answer probably lies in the realistic approach being taken by most authors. From the publication of *Plutach's Lives* to the beginning of this century, biographies were either boringly factual or idealistic to the point that a hero's misdeeds were never revealed. In contrast to this, most author's today strive for accurate reporting of a more comprehensive nature that does not overlook human frailties. Some writers seem obsessed with the latter and apparently take pleasure in defaming cherished national heroes. Other authors have enhanced their works by using reliable, primary source materials which have provided insight into the motives and emotional reactions of great persons during periods of trial. The style of modern biographies has also contributed to their popularity. Today's accounts are streamlined by sharp imagery, animated dialogue and suspenseful situations that build to a climax. Reputable biographers have not sacrificed accuracy in their efforts to fictionalize events.

The endless variety of subjects available in biographies lends enchantment to this form of literature. From childhood, most adults can recall those early tales of America's discovery by Columbus, John Smith's efforts to provide food for the colonists, Washington's leadership that brought us independence, the winning of the West by men such as Daniel Boone, early explorations by Lewis and Clark, and Sacajawea's guidance of the latter which assisted so materially to the success of their expedition. A biographical approach to the study of history lends a personalized touch to this subject. Children are lifted temporarily from their daily routine and into a heroic realm. Like the realistic stories, biographies provide excellent orientation to problems faced by minority group members. Jackie Robinson's rocky road to fame as the first Negro to play in the major leagues is sensitively described in *Breakthrough to the Big League: The Story of Jackie Robinson* by Jackie Robinson and Alfred Ducket. *Frederick Douglass* by Arna Bontemps describes one of the first successful efforts of a black man to provide leadership for his people. Music will take on added meaning through the stories of Beethoven and Mozart by Reba Paeff Mirsky. Both boys and girls will thrill to the excitement of *John H. Glenn: Astronaut* by Lt. Col. Philip Pierce and Karl Schuon. The role of girls in space exploration is told in *Astronaut's Nurse: The Story of Dee O'Hara* by Virginia McDonnell. Fine Stories such as these will inspire children and also help to build a love for literature.

SUMMARY

This chapter has briefly delineated and described several of the traditional types of stories suitable for the raconteur. The four categories discussed were folk literature which included myths, sagas and folk tales; narrative poetry which embraced epics, ballads, story poems and nursery rhymes; realistic stories, and the fourth, biographies. It is hoped that this chapter has provided additional background for storytellers which will facilitate story selection.

---

1. Max J. Herzberg, *Myths and Their Meaning* (Boston: Allyn and Bacon, Inc., 1966) pp.4-5.
2. *Ibid.*, p. 15.

3

Choosing Stories

Shall we permit our children, without scruple,
to hear any fables composed by any authors
indifferently, and so to receive into their minds
opinions generally and reverse of those which,
when they are grown to manhood, we shall
think they ought to entertain?
Plato, *The Republic*

Stories possessing the action, clarity and content that are desirable
for children are not found in every book store. This chapter seeks to
establish guidelines relating to the child, the story and the storyteller
which will facilitate an intelligent choice of material.

THE CHILD

A librarian was once asked by a parent, "What type of story should
I tell my six-year-old son?" Lacking additional information about the
child, the librarian could only reply, "It all depends on the child." An
introverted boy who knocks game-winning home runs only in his imagination might profit from participation stories. An athletically-inclined child
might develop insight into the problem of those who have to struggle to
excel physically if he were to read the life story of Theodore Roosevelt
or Robert Louis Stevenson. If a story's objective is to be realized, it must
be adapted to the individual needs of the child. Teachers and youth
workers who tell stories to groups of children of diverse interests will
find help in the following delineation of specific characteristics of four
age groups. Storytelling parents will also find assistance in the grouping
that matches their child's age.

Age of Repetition

This group includes children from three to six years old. Stories
which contain concrete, familiar objects, talking animals and a repeti-

tious plot will appeal to this age group. "The Three Little Pigs," "Chicken Little," and "The Gingerbread Boy" are examples of such stories. Plots should be simple with a repetitious story line. Plots that demand abstract thinking should be avoided. Tales with characters whose counterparts have been seen by children on trips to the zoo and the countryside will find ready acceptance. Included in stories for this age group should be familiar objects such as dogs, kittens, balls, toys, boats, airplanes, etc. A child's experiences during the age of repetition is heavily dependent upon his five senses. Objects that he has felt, tasted, smelled, heard, or seen, will be welcomed by him in stories. Children in this group are well-acquainted with their own pattern of play activity. Consequently, they respond favorably to stories about themselves or the activities of other children of their own age.

Since youngsters do not enjoy the attention span of an adult, the same picture must be flashed upon their mental screen frequently. The following repetitive taunt of the Gingerbread Boy is enjoyed by three to six-year-olds because of its reassuring nature:

I've run away from a little old woman,
A little old man,
A barn full of threshers,
A field full of mowers,
A cow and a pig,
And I can run away from you, I can!

As these lines are repeated, a child is quickly oriented to the sequence of the story. He is subtly pleased and flattered by his recognition of what has happened to the Gingerbread Boy. He feels secure because he knows which action follows another. He not only enjoys repetition within the story, but also through repeat performances of the same tale. Commenting on this characteristic, Gesell states that a five-year-old" . . . shows preference for certain stories which he likes to hear over and over."[1] Children in the Age of Repetition will accept talking animals, trees and rivers without question. This latter characteristic is by no means limited to children in this group. The message of the talking animal, insect, or bird is the important element. *The Jatakas*, for example, are ancient animal fables sacred to Buddhists. These describe the rebirth of Buddha in various animal incarnations. In the story of *Charlotte's Web*, a loquacious spider provides action for a six-year-old, emotional appeal for a third grader and a lampooning of the shallow values of today's society that will delight high school students. Other talking animals which appeal to more mature listeners and readers may be found in *Dr. Doolittle's Travels, The Wind in the Willows*, and in the mirth-provoking story of Amos, the talking mouse, in *Ben and Me*.

Older children must be prepared for flights of fancy. One children's librarian, who was faced with the assignment of telling stories to mixed groups ranging in age from five to eleven years, began her story by saying, "Boys and girls, we are going to take a journey to the Land of Make-Believe and visit a sister and brother who own a magic horse." This approach called for a willing suspension of disbelief on the part of the older children and also served to eliminate any doubt as to whether the ensuing story was going to be fact or fiction.

Age of Fancy

This group includes children from six to nine years of age. It is a magical period for storytellers and children alike. Creative thinking can be stimulated and desirable character traits strengthened by such tales as Grimm's "The Golden Goose," Filmore's "The Twelve Months," and the Vietnamese tale, "The Sparrow." Stories of this period in the fairy tale category should reward generosity and punish evil-doing and selfishness. Although the immediate effect of a fairy tale is to entertain, the long-term effect of such stories may have moral significance. The child's reaction of approval or disapproval during these vicarious experiences assists him to develop a sense of values. Delightful fantasy may also be found in the *Wizard of Oz, Alice in Wonderland, Winnie the Pooh* and *Peter Pan.* Geeslin's study of current book choices of pupils revealed that *Winnie the Pooh* was the most consistent preference of third graders interviewed? In addition to fairy tales, children in this age group enjoy stories about air travel, science, primitive times, children's classics and religious stories. Most nine-year-olds will also respond to mysteries, biographies and travel adventure.

Age of Hero Worship

This group includes children from nine to twelve years of age. Youngsters in this period like to experience danger, daring, and action from a vicarious vantage point. They will be more attracted to the dashing action of Joan of Arc than to the quiet laboratory experiments of Madame Curie, though both women are heroines. The exploits of a World Series pitcher seem more important than the computations of Albert Einstein. However, both Madame Curie and Albert Einstein belong to the world of storytelling but they demand older audiences. The physical exploits and adventure found in the tales of Robin Hood and King Arthur have timeless appeal. The stories surrounding Tom Sawyer and Huck Finn also belong in this category. Added to these may be the adventures of Beowulf, Hercules, Sir Walter Raleigh, William Tell, Robert the Bruce, Kit Carson and many other heroes of yesteryear.

Gesell has found that ten-year-olds are attracted to stories that have "secret," "mystery," or "horse" in the title.

> Besides horse and dog stories, even sad ones that are going to come out good in the end. Ten likes biographies of famous people, adventure and mystery. Some restrict themselves to stories of their own age and time. Others like to experience children of their own age growing up to become famous people. Historical books are interesting but sometimes they lack enough adventure[3]

Children of this age welcome changes of routine in the school day. Starting with a story, rather than a formalized approach is appreciated. Perhaps a chapter from *Huckleberry Finn* or *The Voyage of Uylsses* would get the day off to a good start. Biographies should personalize great persons and make them seem real. Youngsters welcome incidents that depict their hero's failures as well as his successes. Most children, for example, will sympathize with Herbert Hoover on the occasion when he discovered that he had failed his composition examinations.

Recent research has shed some interesting light on children's literary interest and characteristics in this age group. Steirt designed an inventory to investigate recreational reading interests of pupils in grades five and six. She learned that girls read more books than boys and prefer fiction to non-fiction. Boys, in contrast, choose non-fiction over fiction when they were in the mood to read. Comic books were not mentioned as a reading choice by any of the 285 children studied[4] Burgdorf found that scores on drawing inferences from literary selections were significantly higher when children listened to stories than when they read the stories themselves. The effect of maturation is suggested as the children's ability to draw inferences was significantly higher both in grade five as compared with grade four and in grade six as compared with grade five. There was no significant difference between the scores of boys and girls[5] Storytellers may also benefit from the findings contained in Peltola's study of the literary choices of fourth and sixth grade boys and girls. A sex difference was discernible in the type of favorite characters chosen. Most frequently, the children named characters of their own sex. In second place, boys named animal characters most frequently. Girls named as many male characters as animal characters. Real stories were preferred by more children in both grades than make-believe stories. However, the proximity of fourth graders to the Age of Fancy is probably responsible for their naming make-believe stories as their favorites more often than sixth graders. More children in both grades named recommended books in preference to non-recommended books. However, the sixth graders named fewer recommended books than the fourth graders. This latter finding may suggest the establishment of more independent reading habits by the older children[6]

The conclusions found in the foregoing research will facilitate an intelligent selection of stories for children in the Age of Hero Worship. Many teachers find that the urge for adventure is further satisfied by creatively acting out scenes and short stories. Chapter 5 explains the value of this activity for all ages.

Age of Idealism

This period begins at age twelve and, ideally lasts for the rest of one's life. Stories of adventure which are replete with action, suspense and excitement continue to be popular at this age. Both sexes will show interest in stories which explore vocational and professional areas. Biographies of John Fitzgerald Kennedy, Dwight Eisenhower and Martin Luther King, Jr. are typical materials. Boys will listen to stories about boys but they are cool to *Little Women*, for example. Girls, in contrast to this, will listen to stories about boys and they also enjoy stories of family relations and romance. Girls of thirteen continue to be fond of animal stories, especially those that involve horses. Stories about athletes, with emphasis on fair play, are prized by twelve-year-olds and those in early teens. Stories of primitive peoples, mystery stories and tales of intrigue will also prove popular.

Stanchfield has concluded an enlightening study on the reading interests of eighth-grade boys. Her subject varied in reading ability from superior to poor. Out of the twenty characteristics of stories, excitement, suspense, unusual experiences and surprise or unexpectedness were preferred most frequently. Family love and closeness and familiar experiences were least popular. The most preferred subjects were stories of explorations and expeditions, and outdoor life. These adventure stories tied for first place. Tales of fantasy, life adventure of boys, historical fiction of their own age, sea adventure, sports and games and war followed in that order. Family and home life, plays, art and poetry were last. This study did not bear out the belief that boys at the same grade level with differing reading abilities, will have different reading interests. There were no significant differences in the preferences of superior, average, and poor readers. The boys showed little interest in such qualities as anger, hatred, cruelty, fighting, brutality and sadness. Stanchfield explains,

> War stories had a great appeal for the boys, but only in the idealized sense; they did not care for the brutality, fighting, and horror of war. It was evident that they were highly interested in unusual experiences and not very much interested in familiar, commonplace happenings?

As young people become sex-conscious, both boys and girls normally gravitate toward stories involving boy-girl relations. Teachers, parents and youth workers are faced with the problem of choosing stories for young people in whom elemental passions have begun to stir, yet who lack the self-control and judgment that comes with maturity. A wholesome development of the boy-girl theme takes place in *High Trail* by Vivian Breck. The author portrays the doubts, curiosity, bewilderment and pain of young love and still manages to preserve its rare beauty. Storytellers should be alert for materials that represent the natural attraction of the two sexes within the confines of social acceptability.

THE STORY

Children and Literature

When today's great-grandparents were children, a more leisurely manner of living provided storytelling occasions around cracker barrels in neighborhood stores, in classrooms and within the family circle as its members gathered around a potbellied stove or a crackling hearth fire for an evening's activities. Mark Twain remembered sitting around his Uncle Daniel's fire at John Quarles's farm:

> I can see the white and black children grouped on the hearth, with the firelight playing on their faces and the shadows flickering upon the walls, clear back toward the cavernous gloom of the rear, and I can hear Uncle Dan'l telling the immortal tales which Uncle Remus Harris was to gather into his books and charm the world with, by and by; and I can feel again the creepy joy which quivered through me when the time for the ghost story of the "Golden Arm" was reached—and the sense of regret, too, which came over me, for it was always the last story of the evening and there was nothing between it and the unwelcome bed.[8]

Today's expanded curriculum, children's organizations, radio and television all compete for the precious moments that used to be devoted to reading and listening to stories. Witty reports that in 1965, children spent about twenty hours weekly in front of television sets. In the first grade the average was about fifteen hours; a peak of twenty-five hours was reached in the fifth grade. Pupils in the second grade stated that they spent about three hours each listening to radio; in the fifth and sixth grades the weekly average was about eight hours. He adds,

> It is clear from our studies that the amount of reading of children today is a little greater than in the past. But there are many pupils who read less now, and many others who read very little. Moreover, we should bear in mind that the time devoted to TV, as compared with that given to reading, is very large—about three hours daily to TV and only one hour to reading.[9] The picture is not a bright one in so far as the first "R" is concerned.

Although television is criticized for the inroads it makes into a child's day, it has also earned praise as a means of stimulating viewer's interest in literature. In recent studies, about 25 percent of the elementary school children interviewed claimed that Walt Disney productions had encouraged them to read certain books. Middle grade students credited television and movies with their interest in Tom Sawyer, Mary Poppins, Helen Keller, Little Women, Robin Hood, Heidi and Treasure Island![10] In a television experiment in London, publicity given to twelve authors resulted in increased reading of their works in public libraries![11] The foregoing research suggests that television is capable of lending increased impetus to interest in good literature if a larger percentage of youngsters could be encouraged by their parents to view the most helpful programs. Unfortunately, there seems to be little supervision. Hess and Goldman's research reveals that in the majority of families, the young child watches almost as much as he wishes, and, for the most part, views programs of his own choice. In the majority of families, the mothers make little effort to supervise either program selection of the child or the amount of time devoted to viewing. The father, likewise, exerts little influence in guiding the television behavior of his child![12]

The task of placing good books in the hands of children is further complicated by the large numbers of young people that must be served by classroom teachers and librarians. Individual guidance that would lead to children's classics and other quality literature is in short supply. Too few parents are equipped to assist professional educators with this problem. They are prone to accede to their children's pleading for a poorly-written, easily acquired, gaily-colored book from a supermarket's book section without bothering to look between its covers. Peltola found in her study of children's book choices that the jacket or cover influenced children's selections. As an example, youngsters selected Syd Hoff's *Julius,* on the basis of its cover, before they even opened the book![13] Parents who are in doubt as to which story to select for their child may do well to begin with the time-tested tales that appealed to them when they were children. The wisdom of this procedure is evidenced by Wilson's poll taken of two hundred and seventy-two young children who were interviewed to determine their preference for stories. "The Three Bears" and other children's classics such as "Mother Goose," "Little Red Riding Hood," and "Cinderella" topped the list![14] Geeslin's study of current book choices of pupils disclosed that *Tom Sawyer, Huckleberry Finn* and *Call of the Wild* were among titles popular with older children for forty years![15] Wilson further indicated that factors which influenced the children's responses might have been parents' knowledge of and ability to purchase books combined with the presence or absence of desirable books![16] If parents cannot afford to budget for some of the fine collections of children's stories available on today's market, perhaps the best alternative is to depend on their local library and the reliable advice pertaining to book choice that awaits them there.

Although there is no simple solution to the foregoing problems, they do reinforce the need to present good literature to young people whenever a storytelling opportunity presents itself. Teachers and parents cannot hope to tell *all* of the children's classics, fairy tales, myths, etc., to their young charges. However, by choosing interesting material of literary worth. they may introduce young people to good stories and whet their appetites for more of the same fare. How can one determine if a story is worth telling? Perhaps one of the most satisfactory means of determining the merit of material is to evaluate it according to literary standards.

Literary Worth

Great stories which have survived centuries of appraisal may be found to contain a *universal truth* . . . a message that applies not to one little village or a country but to all of mankind. *Cinderella,* for example, is translated into many languages for it reminds the world that goodness is its own reward; the *Steadfast Tin Soldier* stands firmly in the presence of adversity; *Sleeping Beauty* demonstrates the power of love over evil; and *The Emperor's New Clothes* reveals man's frailty to speak the truth for fear of breaking with convention. A more contemporary example of the powerful use of a universal truth is found in L.M. Boston's *The Stranger at Green Knowe.* A child who had been imprisoned as a refugee identifies with a gorilla which had escaped from a zoo. Both had experienced the frustration of incarceration and both sought freedom . . . a goal which is common to both man and beast. Universals flow like deep rivers through fine literature.

A story possessing literary worth should also have *life-like characters.* "Life-like" does not mean that the characters have actually lived, but they must be convincing. Characters such as Jim and Della in "The Gift of the Magi" are realistic; the husband and wife in "The Three Wishes" are pure fantasy, yet all four are life-like. Storybook personalities may use "cockney" English, slang, or precise, correct grammar depending on their station in life. They must "fit" into the era into which they are cast. The jargon of teenagers does not belong at the conference table of King Arthur and his knights. Parents in stories should react as parents normally do. An unrealistic, highly idealistic portrayal of family relationships is found in "Moving Day" by Earl M. Rush. The father maintained his composure in spite of the trying circumstances that are usually associated with furniture moving. Milk is spilled on his suit, one bedroom slipper is lost, he is constantly questioned by his sons about when the moving van would come, and he caps his performance by lending his wristwatch to his little boy for the balance of the day. The mother permits her children, ages eight and nine years old, to choose and pack kitchen dishes that wouldn't be needed for some time. Children who had never cooked were expected to make these judgments. The moving men were the epitome of patience and the children collided with them and interfered with their work. No one seemed concerned as little sister unpacked boxes that had been carefully packed. Strangely too, the children seemed happy to leave their friends and move to the country. Peterson observes that a normal family would experience fatigue, tension, annoyance, homesickness, etc., during a family move. She also notes that a child reading this story cannot help but wonder why his father does not do such an adequate job of fulfilling his children's fantasies. She states,

> A picture with a few shadows may be healthier and perhaps even less threatening than a blindingly bright one. It should be reassuring for children to realize that a family can remain a solid unit in spite of occasional disagreements and that parents who love their children will still be annoyed with them at times. If we constantly expose children to idealized images of family relationships, most of them must sometimes make an unfavorable comparison between the model we present and the reality of their own home situations. Although we hope many of our students can avoid patterning their adult lives after the unstable or disturbed patterns of their present environment, it is unwise to present them with models which deny a large segment of human experience![7]

Storytellers should select stories that portray the weaknesses and strengths of characters in a life-like manner. This will facilitate the listener's identification with persons in the story.

Another means of judging a story's literary worth is through an examination of an author's *word usage*. Although a storyteller usually does not repeat the identical words of an author when telling stories, an examination of the story will reveal the author's skill at describing accurately, vividly and imparting a smoothly flowing action. Consider Wordsworth's splendid employment of verbs, adjectives, and adverbs in the following excerpt:

I WANDERED LONELY AS A CLOUD

I wandered lonely as a cloud
That floats on high o'er vales and hills,
When all at once I saw a crowd,
A host, of golden daffodils;
Beside the lake, beneath the trees,
Fluttering and dancing in the breeze.

Continuous as the stars that shine
And twinkle on the milky way,
They stretched in never-ending line
Along the margin of a bay:
Ten thousand saw I at a glance,
Tossing their heads in sprightly dance.

Word usage of this nature kindles a child's imagination and deepens his sense of appreciation of nature's wonders.

To be worthy in a literary sense, a story must also possess a *logical plot*. A plot is a story's plan of action, a synthesis of the incidents which happen to the characters. A good plot will produce clear character development and a sequence of action that partitions into distinct episodes. Stories with digressions, subplots, and flashbacks should be avoided for young audiences because of their confusing effects. Following is an example of concise plot construction:

THE FISHERMAN AND HIS WIFE

I. Introduction: A fisherman and his wife live in a pigsty close to the sea. The fisherman catches a magic fish, which was actually an enchanted prince, and returns it to the sea.

II. Rising Action: A. Wife has husband request a cottage from the fish.
B. Wife has husband request a castle from the fish.
C. Wife has husband request that she be made king.
D. Wife has husband request that she be made emperor.
E. Wife has husband request that she be made pope.
F. Wife has husband request that she be made lord of the sun and of the moon. (climax)

III. Conclusion: The fisherman and his wife are reduced to living in a pigsty as they were originally.

This story introduces its conflict situation after a short introduction, it marches directly toward the final resolution of the conflict and concludes quickly after its climax is reached. Stories such as the foregoing that present harmony in their emotional tone, structure, content and word usage are said to have *unity*.

In addition to containing a universal truth, life-like characters, effective word usage and a logical plot, a story must have an *appropriate setting*. Mention was made earlier regarding the inadvisability of mixing modern jargon with the vocabulary of King Arthur's knights. Vocabulary must be appropriate to the setting. Similarly, the setting should be consistent as far as place is concerned. If a story begins in a land of make-believe, its mood would be shattered for children if the locale shifted to the Santa Ana Freeway. Stories should be examined for the artistry proper setting may provide. In the foregoing tale of "The Fisherman and His Wife," Grimm skillfully adjusted the condition of the sea to the mood of the fish. The sea was calm when the cottage was requested but with each subsequent demand, more turbulence was introduced to the setting until, ". . . . all the heavens became black with storm clouds, and the lightenings played, and the thunders rolled; and you might have seen in the sea great black waves, swelling up like mountains with crowns of white foam upon their heads." Effect through setting is also achieved in "Snow White and the Seven Dwarfs" wherein the queen's chemistry laboratory contributes to the feelings of evil surrounding the witch, while the simple, white cottage suggested the innocence and goodness of Snow White and the dwarfs.

A happy blending of literary worth is embodied in "The Elves and the Shoemaker":

I. Introduction: A destitute cobbler and his wife have leather left for but one pair of shoes. He prepares the leather for sewing and retires for the night.

II. Rising Action: A. Cobbler finds completed shoes in the morning. He sells shoes and is able to purchase leather for two pairs, which he cuts.
B. The next morning two completed pairs of shoes await him. The shoes are sold and leather for four pairs of shoes is purchased and cut.
C. Shoemaker and wife sit up and see two elves complete their shoes. They resolve to make clothing for them.
D. Christmas Eve finds the shoemaker and his wife in their hiding place watching the elves as they complete more shoes and find their gifts.

III. Conclusion: Elves dance happily away and the cobbler and wife prosper.

The universal theme in this tale is the power of love. The characters are kindly and generous. They contrast sharply in attitude. The elderly cobbler seems to feel the cares and poverty of a long life but the elves, though threadbare in appearance, seem spritely, spirited and happy.

The use of image-producing words make the four characters seem life-like. The plot is crisp and it is easily followed by children. The mystery of how the shoes were being made is introduced early and the suspense continues even after the elves are observed. The action is cast in the barren, cheerless shop of the shoemaker. This serves as a foil for the prosperity engendered by the elves. The climax is appropriately staged on Christmas Eve . . . a time when many children have thrilled to both giving and receiving gifts. How will the elves react to the surprise planned by the shoemaker and his wife? The ending is happy as the elves dance away into the night.

The foregoing discussion of literary worth of material for storytelling has indicated the importance of a theme that possesses a universal appeal, of characters that seem natural, of word usage that is accurate, smooth and vivid, of a plot that is logical and concise with clear development, and finally, of a setting that is appropriate to the action. Stories with these characteristics contribute to the total effectiveness of a storyteller.

THE STORYTELLER

Identification With the Story

A tale chosen for telling must "fit" both the storyteller and his audience. A raconteur must *identify* with his story. Some material may seem appropriate to one storyteller and foreign to another. Some women feel, without adequate justification, that it takes a man to relate war or sporting-type stories. Preference for tales can frequently be traced to a person's experiences and aptitudes. Followers of the sea will probably be inclined to tell sea stories; woodsmen and mountaineers may find wilderness tales their *forte*. Whatever the choice, the storyteller must feel at ease with his material. He must enjoy his story and must desire to share it with others. Neophyte storytellers will do well to begin with folktales and read at least a half dozen before attempting to make a selection. The story enjoyed most on first reading will probably be a safe choice for telling.

Purpose

Stories are usually selected for a *specific purpose*. All stories should entertain but some are selected solely for that reason. A teacher may wish to instruct by telling her class about the discovery of radium; she may wish to stir interest in professional pursuits by relating the biographies of Dr. Walter Reed, Henry Ford or Clarence Darrow. She may wish to inculcate ideals by describing the character traits displayed by Lou Gehrig, Martin Luther King or Nathan Hale. A teacher might find that children learn obedience more quickly by listening to "Peter Rabbit" than they would by stern admonitions; cleanliness may be incorporated into their behavior patterns more painlessly through hearing of *Angelo, the Naughty One* than through rules, and fear may be dissipated through *Call It Courage.*

Comprehension Level

All who choose stories for young audiences should be alert to the problems that have resulted from a confusion of reading and listening comprehension levels. In an effort to meet the reading needs of youngsters, stories have been categorized into graduated degrees of difficulty known as "reading levels." While there is no intent to criticize the techniques of teaching reading, the result of classification of stories by grade has led to confusion between what a child can read and what a child can listen to successfully. Children have been deprived of many stories within the range of their listening comprehension because these stories have been classified in groups beyond their level of reading comprehension. For example, "Rip Van Winkle" is fascinating listening fare for children in the third grade, and "The Three Sillies" is highly amusing to an audience in the second grade; yet both of these stories are beyond the average reading comprehension of these groups.

Children of today comprehend a great deal more orally than their peers did fifty years ago. Those who work with children should avoid a tendency to "talk down" to them. Youngsters in the kindergarten-primary range watch, in addition to children's television programs, travelogues, documentaries, newscasts and adult movies. According to Nicholson, the vocabulary of kindergarten children in 1967 differs from the vocabulary of the 1926 kindergartner in that the former's vocabulary reflects a wide range of words related to space science, technology and social class values. This research on the oral vocabulary of kindergarten children disclosed that social class was a significant determinant in contrast to sex and race which were not significant determinants of oral vocabulary used by children of this age.[18] An earlier study by Sheehy found similarly that children in 1964 have shifted toward adult responses and norms far more than they did in 1916.[19] The implications for the storyteller are obvious. Not only must vocabulary be geared to a groups' social class generally, but it must challenge six-year-olds who are capable of comprehending far more than their years suggest.

Adult and Child Themes

One of the most common errors of story choice is that of selecting a tale that appeals to an adult with little thought to the interest level of the child. A child may comprehend an adult theme but not be interested in it. A well-meaning individual, swayed one way or the other on a racial problem, for example, might seek out a story on this subject for kindergartners. At this age, most children are "color blind" as far as choice of playmates is concerned. Furthermore, at this age, children would probably prefer "Goldilocks and the Three Bears" to a theme of racial discrimination. In the story-poem, "Little Boy Blue," the same problem may prevail. The story is about a child but it is not for children. Longfellow's reminiscent "The Children's Hour" is appropriate for elderly persons who have raised their families and who enjoy reverie and contemplation of parental experiences. This material should not be force-fed to third graders who crave fairy tales.

Emotional Coloration

Most literary researchers agree that a story's emotional coloration assists listeners and readers to identify with the characters. However, there is a division of opinion as to what constitutes an appropriate act to evoke this emotional response. Kingsley has conducted a critical analysis of the depth and strength of characterization in American children's drama. He contends that some authors espouse happy endings because of the fear of a negative audience reaction to an unhappy ending. Some feel that children need to escape their own sordid surroundings and enter a world of happiness. There is also concern over stunting children's emotional growth due to exposure to adult material. Some educators, allegedly, cling to highly idealistic conditions in stories in their desire to preserve and nurture children's natural moral superiority. Some theologians support the concept of poetic justice and happy endings because of an assumption that a universal and deified system of unerring justice is constantly operating in ultimate reality. Finally, it is believed that some authors and playwrights soften their characterizations because of society's increasing abhorrence of violence and aggression.

In response to these positions, Kingsley explains that new and strange material may be introduced gradually rather than with shocking abruptness. He suggests that it is not so much what is presented but rather how it is done. If children find escape in a world of happiness, they may also find escape in the troubles of others. Most children are believed to be too adaptive to become stunted emotionally by exposure to adult material and their innocence is said to be due to a lack of technique rather than an abundance of virtue. Efforts to depict "rightness" collides with society's conglomeration of confused and conflicting value systems rather than one unified moral code. He further contends, that, theology to the contrary, there are other deities far removed from the deities that children's authorities envision. He points out that happy endings and poetic justice do not happen as often in real life as they do in children's plays and seeks to justify a more realistic approach to this matter:

> It may be that children manifest fright at sudden representation of horror, suffer bad dreams, and for a long time afterward remember the terrifying experience. It also may be that children gain a reinforced pleasure out of imitating the violence which allows them to express their hidden aggressive desires. In any event, the children find the viewing of both pleasurable. However, children's fright need not go unattended, nor must their imitation of aggression become an unfortunate and sometimes deadly carbon copy of the original violent act. It can be rather a "talking out" of the child's fears or a verbal reenactment of the aggression— preferably to the parent who will provide the much needed haven of security the child so often needs.[20]

The results of other research indicate that viewing crime and violence on television is not a crucial determinant of behavior nor of attitudes which might be manifested in behavior. In support of the foregoing, there are indications that such viewing may serve special functions for those who are already socially maladjusted.[21]

A study that produced conclusions which contradicted Kingsley's findings was conducted by Bandura. His experimentation involved nursery children who were divided into three groups. One group watched models perform aggressively, both physically and verbally, toward a large, plastic doll. Another group witnessed subdued behavior of the model toward the doll, while a third group, the control children, were not exposed to the model. Bandura reports:

> Children who observed the aggressive models displayed a great number of precisely imitative physical and verbal responses, whereas such behavior rarely occurred in either the non-aggressive model group or the control group. Children who had observed the aggressive models exhibited approximately twice as much aggression as did subjects in either the non-aggressive model group or the control group. By contrast, children who witnessed the subdued, non-aggressive models displayed the inhibited behavior characteristic of the model and expressed significantly less aggression than the control group.[22]

It is evident from the foregoing that there is need for additional research on this subject. What should be the position of the storyteller in regard to the use of emotional material? How realistic should he be and what influence, if any, should the listener's age have on the selection of material? Perhaps there is a common sense approach to this problem. As far as bedtime storytelling is concerned, most parents put their children to bed to sleep...not to toss and turn. Intelligent parents who possess enough courage to supervise their child's TV viewing will not permit horror-type TV programs, especiallly in the evening hours. Neither will bedtime stories be the nightmare-inducing variety. Admittedly, all TV viewing cannot be supervised and it seems inevitable that some programs will be watched that are probably not in the child's best interests. Parents might also do well to recognize that there is a difference between being horrified and being "properly" frightened. Walter de la Mare, in retrospect, senses the fun and the anticipation of a harmless, scary tale which never lost its emotional flavor for him:

> "...A very small boy may go shivering to bed after listening to the teeny tiny tale of the teeny tiny little woman who found a teeny tiny little bone in the churchyard. The very marrow in his bones may tremble at that final 'Take It." Mine used to; and yet I delighted to have told me again and again by my mother.[23]

Fear is not an emotion to avoid in storytelling, even for the very young. Fear, or perhaps it should be called "respect," for the results of running into the street after a ball, is the reaction that serves to keep many youngsters alive. Stories containing appeals to fear may be chosen but they must be employed with the consummate skill for audience adaptation demanded of successful storytellers.

The amount of sobbing done by preschool children suggests that they are aware that life is not all sweetness and light. However, a liberal representation of stories with happy endings and poetic justice is appropriate from nursery school to the third grade. This is a highly impressionable period during which a child indulges in little abstract thinking. Causal reasoning is at low ebb. It has been indicated that a legitimate aim of storytelling is to instruct. If society is to have order rather than anarchy, youngsters must be conditioned to understand that policemen subdue robbers, and not the reverse of this. Law must be respected. During this period, stories should be told that represent life as it *should* be. Of course, the starkness of reality must be faced by older children both within and without the story. Such books as *The Railroad to Freedom* by Hildegarde Swift, *Southtown* by Lorenz Graham, and *Johnny Tremaine* by Esther Forbes help children to come to grips with life as it is without excessive idealism or didactic moralizing.

SUMMARY

This chapter has explored guidelines relating to the child, the story and the storyteller which will facilitate appropriate choice of stories for telling. It has indicated that children from three to six years of age prefer stories that contain concrete, familiar objects, repetition and talking animals. Six to nine-year-olds enjoy fairy tales especially, but they also will listen attentively to children's classics and stories about elementary technology. Children from nine to twelve years of age prefer mysteries, biographies and travel adventures. From twelve on, youngsters continue to enjoy adventure, sports, biographies, and with maturity, romance.

Storytellers are urged to examine material for its literary worth. Stories possessing the latter contain a universal truth, life-like characters, imaginative, accurate word usage, logical plot and an appropriate setting. Storytellers are urged to choose stories which they enjoy personally. Selection should be made with a definite purpose in mind whether it be to entertain, instruct, or inculcate ideals. Stories should be chosen on the basis of the child's listening, not his reading ability. During children's early years, stories should be selected that represent life as it should be, not as it frequently is. Emotional coloration of a tale should be appropriate to the mental age of the listeners.

1. Arnold L. Gesell and Frances L. Ilg, *The Child From Five to Ten,* New York and London; Harper & Bros., 1946, p. 371.
2. D.H. Geeslin, "A Descriptive Study of the Current Book Choices of Pupils on Three Grade Levels: A Search for the Effects of Reading Age upon Reading Interests," *Dissertation Abstracts,* XXVIII, 1967, p. 875-A.
3. *Gesell,* op.cit., p. 59.
4. Katherine Steirt, "The Designing of an Inventory to Investigate Recreational Reading Interests of Pupils in Grades Five and Six," *Dissertation Abstracts,* XXVIII, 1967, p. 148-A.
5. Arlene Bernice Burgdorf, "A Study of the Ability of Intermediate-Grade Children to Draw Inferences from Selections of Children's Literature," *Dissertation Abstracts,* XXVII, 1966, p. 2003-A.
6. Bette Jean Peltola, "A Study of the Indicated Literary Choices and Measured Literary Knowledge of Fourth and Sixth Grade Boys and Girls," *Dissertation Abstracts,* XXVII, 1966, p. 609-A.
7. Jo M. Stanchfield, "The Reading Interests of Eighth-Grade Boys," *Journal of Developmental Reading,* Summer, 1962, pp. 256-265.
8. Mark Twain's Autobiography, Vol. 1, Harpers, New York, 1924, p. 112.
9. Paul Witty, "Children of the Television Era," *Elementary English,* 44, p. 529-531.
10. Ibid., 530.
11. *Times* Editorial Supplement, 2710:1435, "Television and the Reader," April 28, 1967.
12. Robert D. Hess and Harriet Goldman, "Parents' Views on the Effect of Television on Their Children," *Child Development* 35, June, 1962, 424.
13. Bette J. Peltola, "A Study of Children's Book Choices," *Elementary English,* 40:690— 695, November, 1963.
14. Frank T. Wilson, "Stories That Are Liked by Young Children," *The Journal of Genetic Psychology,* 1943,63, 68-69.
15. D. H. Geeslin, "A Descriptive Study of the Current Book Choices of Pupils on Three Grade Levels: A Search for the Effects of Reading Age Upon Reading Interests," *Dissertation Abstracts,* XXVIII, 875-A.
16. Wilson, *op. cit.,* 68-69.
17. Barbara G. Peterson, "Life Maladjustment Through Children's Literature," *Elementary English* 40: November, 1963, 718.
18. Elsie Mae Nicholson, "An Investigation of the Oral Vocabulary of Kindergarten Children from Three Cultural Groups with Implications for Readiness and Beginning Reading Programs," *Dissertation Abstracts,* XXVII, 1966, 710-A.

19. Sister Mary Serena Sheehy, "A Developmental and Normative Study of Word Associations in Children Grades One Through Six," *Dissertation Abstracts*, XXVI, 484, July 1965.
20. W.H. Kingsley, "Happy Endings, Poetic Justice and the Depth and Strength of Characterization in American Children's Drama: A Critical Analysis," *Dissertation Abstracts*, XXVI, 1965, 3534-3535.
21. Joseph T. Klapper, *The Effects of Mass Communication*, Glencoe, Illinois, The Free Press of Glencoe, 1960.
22. Albert Bandura, "Behavioral Modifications Through Modeling Procedures," L. Krasmer and L.P. Ullman, *Research in Behavior Modification*, New York: Holt, Rinehart, and Winston, 1965.
23. Walter de la Mare, *Animal Stories*, New York: Scribner, 1939.

4

The Story:
Its Preparation
and Presentation

PREPARING THE STORY

Suggestions for an intelligent choice of a story have been discussed in Chapter 3. The storyteller has made her selection with a definite purpose in mind. She intends to meet the need of a child or group by instructing, character building or entertaining. The story has literary worth, and is loaded with action and suspense, which is appropriate to the age level of her group. After selecting the story, the next step is to prepare it for telling. An effective oral story must be characterized by a short introduction; a body that moves directly toward the climax without any betrayal of what the latter is going to be; and finally, a brief conclusion.

Introduction

An effective introduction must motivate children to listen, establish the mood of the story and present the conflict situation. Children are delighted to listen if a personal relationship is established between them and the story's characters. A teacher may say, "Today, boys and girls, I would like to share a problem faced by a boy named Freddie. You have probably had a similar decision to face. Let us see if Freddie's solution is the one you would have chosen." Now that the children's attention has been captured, mood may be established by various devices. Time may be used to waft children off to the land of yesteryear. "Once upon a time, long before there were automobiles, telephones, radios or television sets, a little boy was born in a log cabin in Kentucky." Emotional appeal is frequently employed to build mood e.g. "Once upon a time there lived a little girl who was so poor that she had neither shoes on her feet nor a warm coat to shield her from a bitter wind." Mood may also be created by the attitude of the storyteller. Listeners will be prone to believe that a story is funny, adventurous, serious or tragic if the narrator believes it to be so. In addition to developing the audience's desire to listen and building mood, the introduction should pique interest by presenting the problem, the conflict upon which the story must grow. In the following stories, a conflict situation is introduced in the first sentence and listeners immediately become party to the action:

"How the Camel Got His Hump" by Rudyard Kipling
In the beginning of years, when the world was so new and all, and the Animals were just beginning to work for Man, there was a Camel, and he lived in the middle of a Howling Desert because he did not want to work: and besides, he was a Howler himself."

"Thumbelina" by Hans Christian Andersen

There was once a woman who had the greatest longing for a little tiny child, but she had no idea where to get one; so she went to an old witch and said to her, "I do so long to have a little child, will you tell me where I can get one?"

No time is lost in the first tale describing how a desert looks or what a camel is; in the second story the author ignores any description of the old lady and instead, plunges directly into the plot. Children wait expectantly for action and they must be given it. Not all stories have introductions as ideally suited for storytelling as the foregoing examples. However, through a judicious elimination of unnecessary material, storytellers may create introductions that command attention, set the mood of a story and present the conflict situation.

The Body

Following the preparation of the introduction, a storyteller should reread the story to seek out the ideas that belong together. When the reader begins to see a relationship of thought groups, the story's *key situations* become evident. Key situations are actually minor climaxes which lead to the high point or the main climax of a poem or story. Each key situation has a purpose. It may build character, intensify tragedy, provide relief from tension, or speed the tempo toward the climax. Following are the key situations in Russell Herman Conwell's "Acres of Diamonds":

a. A Buddhist priest visits Al Hafed, the wealthy one, and describes a diamond.
b. Al Hafed is determined to find diamonds.
c. Al Hafed disposes of property and family.
d. Al Hafed searches for the precious stones.
e. Al Hafed, in poverty, commits suicide. (key situation which is also the climax)
f. New owner finds diamonds on the farm which Al Hafed had sold him. (anti-climax and conclusion)

After it has been determined where a climax occurs, a teacher should keep this uppermost in mind as she practices the story aloud. She should subordinate key situations to it but continue to build tension and suspense until her preparation reaches the point where listeners are startled by the high point in a story. In "Acres of Diamonds," an audience would know that Al Hafed's fortune is on the downgrade but the story keeps alive the possibility that the once-rich Al Hafed might stumble upon wealth. This hope is dashed at the high and terrible moment when the luckless one hurls himself into the sea and ends his quest. The body of the story develops the conflict situation established in the introduction. Key situations carry the listeners with mounting interest to the climax which signals the conclusion of the tale.

Conclusion

Like the introduction, the conclusion should be characterized by brevity. At this point, the climax has been reached, audience interest has peaked and begun to wane and prolongation only serves to lessen the impact of the story. Note how quickly the following stories have been concluded after their climax has been reached: "How the Coyote Danced with the Blackbirds" is a Zuni legend which ends immediately after the coyote's failure to fly, with the statement, "Therefore, you will often meet coyotes to this day who have little black fringes along the rear of their forelegs, and the tips of their tails are often black. Thus it was in the days of the ancients." In "Gudbrand on the Hillside" the husband commits the grossest of errors only to be praised by his wife. The folktale concludes immediately thereafter with Gudbrand opening his door and saying to his neighbor who had been a silent witness to the scene, "Have I won the hundred dollars now?" The neighbor was obliged to confess that he had. The apex of interest in each of the foregoing stories had been reached, the impact had been made on the listeners, and prolongation with moralizing by a storyteller would only lead to a laboring of the obvious.

General Considerations

Cue Cards: Many storytellers find a cue card beneficial. It is a skeleton outline of a story which includes the title, author, source, the time required for telling, the names of the separate characters, the scenes to indicate change in time and/or place and a brief synopsis of the plot. The use of cue cards is usually preferred to the painstaking memorization of stories that involves a prodigious amount of time. For most individuals, memorization stands in the way of a spontaneous, uninhibited presentation. It limits immediate adaptation to an audience which is one of the primary virtues of storytelling. Furthermore, the verbatim method of preparation also increases the possibility of speech fright in a story-teller. If the teacher concentrates on the specific language of an author, a momentary lapse of memory becomes infinitely more upsetting than if the plot and characters had been the primary items of study. Cue cards will encourage teachers to tell stories they normally would be inclined to read to their classes. They should be used inconspicuously so as not to detract from the story. Storytellers are urged to develop card files of useful stories which may be quickly reviewed for telling. 4" x 6" cards are a functional size for this purpose. Following are typical examples of cue cards:

Title: "Talk" (African folk tale)
Author: Harold Courlander and George Herzog
Source: *The Bookshelf for Boys and Girls,* The University Society, New York, 1958, IV, p. 85.
Time: Five Minutes
Characters: The farmer, the fisherman, the weaver, a man bathing, the Chief.
Scenes: Farm, road, river, house of the Chief.

Synopsis: Once, in the country of Guinea, a farmer went out into his garden to dig up some yams to take to market. One of the yams said, "Leave me alone." The farmer looked around to see who had spoken, and his dog said, "The yam said to leave him alone." The farmer became angry and cut a branch from a palm tree to whip the dog. The palm said, "Put that branch down." The farmer was about to throw it away when the branch said, "Put me down gently." He put the branch on a stone, and the stone said, "Take that thing off me." This was enough—the frightened farmer started running for his village. He met a fisherman carrying a fish trap. He told his story, and the fisherman was unmoved until his fish trap said, "Well, did he do it?" Then they ran together toward the village. They met a weaver carrying a bundle of cloth. They told him their story. The weaver couldn't understand their fright until his cloth said, "You'd be frightened too!" All three men ran until they met a bather in the river and told their story. The bather couldn't understand why they were running until the river said, "You'd run too!" They all ran to the house of the Chief, who brought his stool out, sat down, and listened to their story. When they were through he scolded them and sent them back to work. He said to himself, "Nonsense like that upsets the village." "Fantastic, isn't it? his stool said. "Imagine a talking yam."

Title: "The Baker's Neighbor" (Peruvian folk tale)
Author: Translated by Frank Henuis
Source: *The Bookshelf for Boys and Girls,* The University Society, New York, 1958, IV, p. 218.
Time: Five or six minutes.
Characters: A baker, his neighbor, a judge.
Scenes: A bakery, a street, a courtroom.

Synopsis: Once in Lima, Peru, there lived a very industrious baker who loved money. His neighbor was the opposite, and each morning loved to smell the freshly baked bread. The greedy baker thought he should pay for this daily aroma and asked him to do so. The man laughed and before long the whole town was laughing. The baker took the case to court. The judge ordered both men to appear and told the neighbor to bring a bag filled with 100 gold coins. It appeared the judge was going to make him pay. In court, the baker told his story and the neighbor admitted that he did enjoy the aroma. The judge took the money and handed it to the baker, asking him to count the money to be sure it was all there. Then the judge arose and announced his decision: "I hereby declare that this case is now settled, baker. Your neighbor has smelled your pastry, and you have seen and touched his gold. The case is dismissed."

Cutting: Storytellers find material, occasionally, that lacks appropriate construction, contains irrelevant ideas, or is too lengthy for the amount of time allotted for the story period. Under these circumstances, it is permissible to eliminate portions of a story provided the *intent of the author is not changed.* In "The Little Red Hen," for example, the goose or the duck could be eliminated. The time spent describing the trip to the mill and details of the miller's conversation could be condensed without changing the moral of the story. Similarly, if the teacher were taking a portion of Irving's "Legend of Sleepy Hollow" for telling, she might eliminate or compress many of the author's lengthy, involved descriptions of the landscape without altering the mood of the story or its plot. Facility in cutting stories comes with practice. Storytellers are urged to perfect this aspect of story preparation because it will admit literature into the story hour which otherwise might go untold.

Building Mood: In earlier pages it has been recommended that beginning storytellers will find their storytelling debut easier if they select a story that they enjoy and one that deals with a subject they understand. Following its selection, the story should be reread for thorough comprehension. Knowing the story implies more than simply scanning the material. It indicates that the criteria for choosing stories has been applied. Every character and every scene is visualized clearly. The more effectively mood is built when preparing a story, the easier it will be to recapture the proper feelings when telling the story. Mood can be developed in the following ways:

1. An understanding of the trials and joys in an author's life may strengthen one's storytelling ability. Knowing the circumstances that prompted an author to write a selection frequently results in a more sympathetic identification by the teller. Edgar Allan Poe's various afflictions haunt his writings. Milton wrote authoritatively on blindness because he had been blind. Robert Frost knew the sound of

whining wood saws and the appearance of birches "ridden down" by a young boy because he had lived on a farm and knew the life intimately. In a mysterious and exciting way, the building of atmosphere and mood begins with the author.

2. Recalling personal experiences that demanded or elicited the same mood as those evidenced in the story will help speed the storyteller into a proper frame of mind. If the mood is light and fanciful, it will help to think of a happy time such as a party, a humorous situation, or the moment when a cherished gift caused delight. Transfer of that mood to the reading of a story will enhance its presentation.

3. Understanding the setting is mandatory. An appreciation of Switzerland's topography and her customs will help one make Heidi's experiences come alive. If one plans to tell a sea story, it might prove helpful to visit the docks and the seashore to"absorb" atmosphere.

4. Identification with situations and characters in a story may be hastened by acting out as much of the tale as possible. This may be done in the privacy of one's study. The storyteller might simulate digging for pirate gold until the shovel strikes a metallic object or perhaps "dancing" with a prince will turn "Cinderella" into a more believable character.

5. All meanings must be clear. Mood is dependent upon understanding every paragraph, every sentence and every word. Only then may the author's words be paraphrased with accuracy.

6. Suspense has been mentioned as an indispensable ingredient in almost every worthwhile story. Nothing creates more immediate suspense than a calculated pause by a storyteller. Pauses should be observed during rehearsals in precisely the same manner that they will be employed when children sit expectantly before their teacher. In the familar story, *Ferdinand,* the principal character has a marvelous entrance into the bullring. The crowd is in a state of frenzy, the trumpets blare and the matadors march. Then an expectant hush falls over the stadium as Ferdinand is released. Here the teacher may pause as the children wonder, "What is Ferdinand going to do?" "Will he get hurt?" Ferdinand charges into the ring. The picadores and the matador eye him warily . . . At this point the tension and suspense will be heightened by another pause. The subsequent action by Ferdinand becomes all the more ludicrous because of the intense build-up which had been dramatized and sharpened by pauses. From the foregoing, it is evident that a pause before an idea or an action builds suspense. What is the effect of a pause after an idea or action has been expressed? Pausing after an idea strengthens the effect of the thought and enables listeners to adjust to approaching dramatic events.

For example, one may say, "A manned space craft has just landed on Mars." A pause at this point will magnify the importance of this pronouncement. Listeners may be prone to ruminate, "What have they found?" "Is there any indication of life?" "Can the ship return?" The pause has dignified the idea and captivated the attention of the audience. Use of a dramatic pause before and after ideas, when done artfully, lends enchantment to storytelling. A storyteller must remember that a pause may seem like an eternity when relating a tale but to children hearing the story, the period is but a twinking. Practice will reveal the importance of this technique.

Dialogue: The use of conversation when storytelling enables a raconteur to identify more closely with characters and permits listeners to feel that an event described is actually taking place. The following selections should be compared noting in one the impersonal quality of straight narration and in the other, the vital, animating effect produced by dialogue:

"Androcles and the Lion"

Narration: Androcles, a runaway slave, had fled to a forest for safety. He had not been there long when he came upon a lion that was groaning with pain. At first Androcles was frightened but the lion made no move to attack him. Emboldened by this, Androcles approached close to the beast and noticed that his paw contained a thorn which he carefully removed. In gratitude, the lion brought the man food. Before many days, however, both the lion and Androcles were captured by Roman soldiers and taken to the city of Rome. Here, according to custom, the slave was condemned to death by fighting a lion in a public arena. The lion had been long without food to increase its ferocity. Thousands of Romans including the Emperor gathered to watch the event. The lion sprang into the amphitheater and Androcles entered from the other end. The beast rushed toward the slave and then, instead of attacking, fawned at the man's feet and licked his hands. The Emperor was amazed and called Androcles before him. When the latter had told his story, the Emperor freed both the slave and the lion. He thought such kindness and such gratitude were deserving of reward.

Dialogue: Many, many years ago, a slave named Androcles escaped from his cruel master and ran into the deep forest for safety. When he was sure that he was far enough into the forest to be hidden from his pursuers, he sat down against a big rock to rest.

Androcles had barely caught his breath when, from behind the very rock on which he was sitting, came a tremendous roar.

"Arr, Arr, Arr," snarled a huge lion who was crouched behind the rock.

Now, just like any of us would do, Androcles started to run from the lion as fast as his legs would carry him. But the lion did not run after him! Androcles, just like any of us, soon became curious and crept back to see why the lion did not follow him.

The lion had not moved from behind the rock. When he saw Androcles returning, he no longer roared at him. Instead, he held up one paw, just like a dog who wants to shake hands.

"What is the matter, my friend?" Androcles asked, as he took the lion's paw in his hand. "Why, you have a thorn in your paw, and the flesh is all torn and bloody. Here, let me pull it out."

Androcles pulled very carefully and out came the thorn!

"Now, my friend," said Androcles, "you can again run free in the forest." But the grateful lion stayed with Androcles, protected him from the dangers of the woods, and brought him food.

One day the lion did not return from a hunting trip. On the same afternoon a band of soldiers captured Androcles and took him to a prison in Rome.

The slave was put on trial. The Emperor said to him, "You have broken the law of the land by running away from your master. You will have to die in the arena where you will be thrown to a hungry lion."

Immediately Androcles was taken into the arena. The crowd sat forward in their seats. All was quiet. Then a great roar came from one end of the amphitheater as a lion was released from his cage. He raced toward Androcles, stopped, crouched ready to pounce, and then sat on his haunches and lifted his paw.

"It is my friend of the forest," said Androcles, who had been certain he was about to be killed. "My friend, you have saved my life."

The Emperor, who was seated in his box near the floor of the arena, commanded Androcles to come to him. The lion followed Androcles to the Emperor's seat like a faithful dog.

"Slave," said the Emperor, "This lion has not been fed for five days, yet he refuses to attack you. Can you tell me why?"

"Your Majesty," said Androcles, "when I escaped into the forest, I removed a thorn from the bloody paw of this same lion. He protected me in the forest and brought me food, and now he has spared my life."

The Emperor arose from his seat.

"Androcles," he said, "you and this beast have taught all of us a lesson in kindness and gratitude. You may both go free."

From that day on, most men have been kind to animals, and those of us who especially love animals have been called lion-hearted.

The foregoing example illustrates the value of dialogue to story-tellers. Characters become more life-like, more believable, and the raconteur is given an opportunity to enhance his presentation.

Delivery: The spoken word may indicate the level of one's education, the degree of friendliness and sincerety, and it may also suggest the amount of time and effort expended in preparation. When a story is practiced aloud the first time, a hesitant, stilted presentation is to be expected. The speaker gropes for words and struggles to remember the sequence. However, with practice, clumsy phrasing and unnecessary repetitions disappear and fluency is achieved. Through love of children and enjoyment of materials chosen for telling, teachers should strive for the cultivation of a warm, friendly, confidential tone. The latter indicates to every child in the class, "This is just for us." Storytellers occasionally misinterpret the meaning of the confidential tone and as a result, tell tales in a semi-whisper. A half-heard story is a strain for youngsters, as well as adults. It is comparable to a television set with its volume turned just below the level for easy listening. If a story is to be fully enjoyed, it must be easily heard.

In addition to using proper volume, storytellers should strive for distinct, correct speech. A teacher's articulation and pronunciation is more likely to be imitated by her pupils than any characteristic of her speaking. A model of good speech is not one who carefully and accurately enunciates and isolates every syllable of a word. Excessive precision has no place in any classroom because it does not constitute standard speech. On the other hand, the teacher who constantly says, "an" for "*and*," "git" for "*get*," "jist" for "*just*," "gonna" for "*going to*," "didja" for "*did you*," and who connects her sentences with "an uh" or vocalizes every pause with "uh" constitutes a threat to the healthy speech development of elementary grade children. Additionally, a storyteller's grammar must be correct. Words used and the manner in which they are applied are measures of a speaker. Saying, "I done," "They was," or pronouncing "modern" "modren" has a detrimental effect. Applied to storytelling, an awareness of these practices places a teacher on guard against articulatory omission, substitutions and inaccuracies. To promote desirable speech habits does not mean that all dialect, colloquialisms, or "street articulations" should be excised from stories. As long as these traits are identified with story characters they may be retained.

Storytellers should also strive for a pleasing, expressive, inflectional pattern. Monotony of inflection must be avoided. The latter may be of the "plateau" type which runs along without appreciable inflectional change or it may be the "bishop's tone" type which repeats the same inflectional pattern over and over again. Monotony of either kind will destroy a presentation of the finest story ever written. Unless a person is habitually monotonous both in everyday conversation as well as in a storytelling situation, monotony may be traced to an emotional indifference to what is being said. Basic to the development of variety in storytelling is an appreciation of the importance of full identification with material being presented. Suggestions made earlier for mood development will assist to combat monotony. A key to variety in speaking is found in the statement, "Impression precedes and determines expression." A reader's impression from the idea on the printed page comes first. This is followed by the reader's mental reaction expressed inflectionally which influences children when a story is told. An expressive voice puts life into a story or poem.

Finally, storytellers should monitor their rate of speaking to be certain that it is appropriate to content. Events within a story are the prime determinants of the speed of delivery. The mood and action of a tale will stimulate a teacher who is sympathetically identified with her material to respond appropriately. A story which depends upon pathos for much of its effectiveness will be delivered more slowly than a story which is fundamentally comic in theme. Individuals usually speak more slowly when they are sad than when they are happy.... because something has stimulated them to *feel* that way. "Cinderella," "The Fir Tree" and "Sleeping Beauty" are three stories that will be characterized by periods of rather slow delivery. In contrast to these, comic tales such as "The Tale of Peter Rabbit," "Pelle's New Suit" and "The Husband Who Was To Mind The House," depend for their effectiveness upon a buoyant interpretation. The storyteller's reaction to events in the story result in a spritely rate of presentation.

Gesture: In order to have rehearsal periods prepare storytellers as fully as possible, it is recommended that final practice be conducted before a full-length mirror. The latter will provide a reasonable amount of distraction which is comparable to that caused by an audience and it will also let a speaker see herself as children will. "How much should I gesture?" is a question commonly asked by beginning storytellers. This question may be answered in part by explaining the relationship of the storyteller to characters in stories. A raconteur should *interpret* a tale. She does not have to act the role of the several characters. Her primary role is to convey an author's intended impressions in such a manner that her audience always sees the story... not the storyteller's performance. More simply stated, she will not simulate tree climbing, riding a witch's broomstick, talk like a squeaky mouse, or drop to her knees in prayer if story characters do these things. Any overt action which transfers attention from a story's content to a storyteller is to be avoided. Speaking before a mirror will also assist to eliminate any nervous, non-meaningful mannerisms such as fingering a necklace, earpulling, needlessly adjusting clothing, and the tiresome, one-arm pump handle gesture. All stories should have gestures but the latter should be subtle. When preparing a story, a teacher will not write such instructions as "Smile here," "Raise voice," or "Clench right fist," in the margin as guides to storytelling. Such reactions must arise with spontaneity and sincerity from the stimuli found in the story. Included would be appropriate facial reactions, perhaps a slight shrug of the shoulders to indicate indifference, or a circular motion of an upraised hand to describe a staircase in a mystery story. If gestures are so much a part of the story that an audience is unaware of them, then a storyteller has made them effectively and desirably.

Use of a tape recorder during rehearsal periods usually proves advantageous inasmuch as it gives a raconteur some idea of the aural impression she is going to make on her audience. Exercises found in the appendix may also prove helpful when used with a tape recorder.

TELLING THE STORY

Physical Arrangement

Once a good story has been chosen and thoroughly prepared, every effort should be made to insure easy reception by children. The storyteller must be certain that room lighting is adequate. She should place the children so that window light is to their backs and not in their faces. Every child should be able to see the speaker without having to peer around the head of the boy or girl in front of him. Chairs need to be spaced to prevent the backs from becoming footrests. If children remain at their desks during the story, every item of school work should be cleared away before the story is told. Pencils, crayons, paper, books and scissors should be left behind if the group moves to chairs or mats for the occasion. As a wise teacher once said before starting a story, "Leave everything behind except your imaginations." Environmental distractions should be avoided. If a jet plane passes over a school at a regular time each day, that period should not be used for storytelling. Eye catchers should be eliminated from the presentation. For example, a story should not be told in front of a bulletin board with brightly colored posters. If a chalkboard is behind the storyteller, it should be erased before beginning the story. Another distraction might well be clothing or accessories worn by the storyteller. Excessive makeup, inappropriate apparel, flashy jewelry or dangling earrings are capable of shifting a child's attention away from the story and to the storyteller. The narrator should seat the audience in front of her, using short, crescent-shaped rows with staggered chair arrangement. Sitting in a circle poses the problem of placing the teacher in a position where she cannot be readily seen by children on either side. Children with behavior problems should be seated near the teacher. The magic of the story may be enhanced by creating a "story corner" in the classroom. Formal seating arrangements would be left behind as the group assembles. As long as behavior is appropriate, friends may sit with friends during the journey to make-believe land. The "story corner" needs only chairs and a table or a shelf for the children's favorite books. This rather barren environment provides the best atmosphere for concentration on the storyteller's message.

Time of Day for Storytelling

A good story, well told, will have an eager audience at any hour of the school day. Some children have requested that their day begin with a story. Teachers have found the following times advantageous: (1) just prior to, or immediately following recess; (2) just prior to or immediately following lunch; and (3) just prior to the end of the school day. Stories presented immediately before recess, lunch, or the close of the school day provide relief from fatigue. Stories told just after recess or lunch provide a means of bringing children to attention quickly and these stories also facilitate classroom control. The foregoing suggestions do not relate to stories employed for instructional purposes. Of necessity, the latter would be told during the regular period of subject matter instruction.

Posture of a Storyteller

A storyteller should be concerned about her posture when storytelling. This may be governed by a number of factors including the age of the children, the content of the story, the size of the class, the length of the story, the time of day, the purpose of telling the story and the comfort of the teacher. There are no hard-and-fast rules for the storyteller's physical position except to point out that poor posture is unbecoming in any situation. To stand while storytelling allows a teacher to judge audience reaction to the fullest degree. It also allows for more freedom of movement. In general, the standing position provides easier vision for all listeners, and is an aid to voice projection. This stance has some limitations. Most teaching is done from a standing position and the story period, apart from teaching, should be developed as something "special." Secondly, there may be an attendant desire to act out the several roles of a story, and, lastly, the confidential atmosphere of story sharing may be difficult to achieve in a standing (or lecture) position. If this position is preferred, the storyteller should not stand behind a chair or a desk. These stand in the way of full sharing and act as a barrier to empathy. By comparison with the foregoing, if a story is told from a sitting position, with the audience seated, the psychological barrier of the teacher-student situation is greatly reduced. The intimacy of the group is increased. Sitting while storytelling will also aid a teacher who is self-conscious about her hands. During her first stories she may simply fold them on her lap. The sitting position will probably be preferred by kindergarten-primary age children who are accustomed to hearing stories related by a seated reader or storyteller. Sitting, however, may impair visual communication in a large group. Some children may not be able to see the storyteller and voice projection might be a problem. For some teachers, sitting on a desk provides a happy ground between sitting and standing. She can see every pupil and be seen by them. Gestures can be used easily and projection is enhanced. On the other hand, this position may encourage a slouched posture and a feeling of too much informality. It may be interpreted by some children as an endorsement of the right to sit on furniture not designed for this purpose. If a teacher speaks from this vantage point, she should explain why she is doing it. The children should understand that the desk is used in this way only during the story period.

Audience Adaptation During the Story

Earlier in this book, the importance of choosing an appropriate story for a given age group was stressed. During storytelling, audience adaptation continues and it may be defined as the storyteller's adjustment to responses of the audience. It includes a continuing evaluation of whether an audience can hear what is being said, whether it can identify itself with what is taking place. Because a teacher usually knows her class members well and because she practices adaptive techniques in her teaching of subject matter, only two suggestions for increasing rapport during storytelling will be made: (1) Danger signals in the form of unrest and mischief may indicate that a story is not "getting through" to a pupil. Sometimes a distracted child can be "recaptured" by saying, "And Johnny, at that moment a wonderful thing happened!" This approach personalizes the story for Johnny, flatters him and regains his attention. The narrator is able to pick up the thread of the story with the minimal amount of correction. (2) Storytellers are urged to use rhetorical questions as attention getters provided they do so wisely. If, in a story, Mary is established as one who assists her mother with house cleaning and baking, the storyteller may inquire, "Mary was a helpful girl, wasn't she?" with little danger of irresponsible or negative chorus answers. However, general questions can lead to disaster. Difficulty awaits the teacher who asks, "Now, what do you suppose Tom received on his birthday?" The likely avalanche of divergent responses would consume the balance of the period and destroy the value of the story.

If more than one story is told during a session, stories should be adapted to the prevailing mood of the children as closely as possible. An excellent example of this is found in youth camps where storytelling takes place around a campfire. When the fire is high, lively, humorous stories are in order; when the flames sink low, when the group quiets, when noises from the forest occasionally penetrate the campfire ring ... then bring on a mystery story!

READING THE STORY

Some stories depend so completely on their language for their effectiveness that they should be read, not told to children. Unless a teacher is willing to devote many hours to perfecting dialects, she will probably do better to read such stories as the Irish Fairy Tale, "King O'Toole and His Goose," and Harris' "Adventures with Uncle Remus." There are also stories by authors with inimitable styles such as Kipling and Scott. Tales by these authors sometimes lose their appeal when they are told instead of read. Lastly, there is a vast supply of story poems which can serve many different purposes in a classroom. Unless a teacher has time to memorize, she will do well to read "I Hear America Singing" to illustrate the American heritage; "King Robert of Sicily" to supply an example of humility; or "The Walrus and the Carpenter" to share just for fun.

Many of the suggestions for preparing and presenting stories apply to reading stories as well as telling them. However, story readers are faced with problems that are unique to this activity. The following additional suggestions should prove helpful:

1. A teacher must encourage the concept of sharing mentioned earlier. The book must not be a barrier between a reader and her listeners thereby causing a teacher to read *to* her children and not *with* them. It is helpful to pretend that the book is held aloft before the children by some magical means, with words pouring mysteriously from it. Where would the teacher be? She would be seated with her children, enjoying the story. The concept of sharing the material permits a teacher to laugh or be sad with the children when a story prompts these reactions. Although a reader must sit or stand before a class and make a printed page come alive by her re-creation of characters and vitalization of scenes, mentally she is in the audience enjoying the story.
2. The manner in which a book is held during oral reading may have considerable influence on the interest and attention of those listening.

A book should not be held so high that it obscures all or part of the face, neither should it be held so low that the reader's chin rests on her chest. A teacher should hold her book at such an angle that eye contact is made easily without excessive up-and-down head movement.

3. One of the obvious disadvantages of story-reading is a loss of some of the eye contact enjoyed by storytellers. This can be compensated in part if a systematic approach is used to establish visual contact with listeners. Looking from book to audience should not be a furtive, slipshod, catch-as-catch-can procedure but rather a well-formulated technique. A reader should develop the habit of looking up from a page upon completion of a thought. This usually occurs at a semicolon or a period. This procedure is rule-of-thumb and must be tempered with common sense. Some story poems, for example, are composed of many short, four-or-five word sentences. When presenting material of this sort, it would be acceptable to look up at the end of every other sentence. Frequent bobbing of the head to establish eye contact is distracting. Eye contact with an audience should be made approximately four or five words from the end of a sentence. This procedure will eliminate looking up, in random fashion within a line. Looking up indiscriminately may be likened to writing commas in lines where they do not belong. Underlining in the following sentence is an example of the point at which a reader's attention might leave the printed page and communicate directly with her audience.

> The old man gathered his meager possessions, closed
> the cupboard, walked from the cabin, and left his
> boyhood home forever.

When a reader looks up from a book her glance should be meaningful . . . . she must want to communicate directly. It should grow out of her desire to share an idea upon its completion. Eye contact should not be a fleeting, furtive action from the book, to the audience in general, and then back to the book. Instead, as a reader looks up, ready to utter the final words of a sentence, she should pick out one member of the group and complete the thought to him. A different child, seated in another part of the room will be singled out to receive eye contact each time the latter is effected. This procedure personalizes the presentation and makes children feel as if they were being read to individually. Eye contact of this type also helps to "steady" restless or mischievous children. Readers also find that looking up at the end of a sentence systematically, rather than looking up randomly, facilitates finding one's place easily upon glancing back to the book. Additionally, eye contact at the end of a sentence, when accompanied by a pause, permits a reader to collect herself for presentation of the idea contained in the next sentence. Finally, if a reader is prone to have stage fright, this systematic method of eye contact will prove reassuring. Indecision of any kind in a speaking situation is conducive to fright and confusion. Knowing when contact is to be made and practicing this technique until it is accomplished automatically will assist a teacher to develop poise and confidence.

Rhythm is a characteristic of all literature, both prose and verse. In prose, the pattern of movement results partly from the idea and partly, but to a lesser degree, from the arrangement of words. In verse, the meter determines rhythm and the idea provides the basis for variety. One of the besetting fears of some readers is that their presentations will be "sing-song." When reading to kindergarten and primary grade children, a reader should not worry if rhythm is prominent and strong. Rhythm is probably the first characteristic of verse that attracts children. They like its swing. Their appreciation of rhythm would probably continue if, when they begin to read, they were not criticized for being "sing-song." When reading the following Mother Goose rhyme, the beat should predominate.

> Ride a cockhorse to Banbury Cross
> To see an old lady upon a white horse;
> Rings on her fingers and bells on her toes,
> She shall have music wherever she goes.

Children will sit and sway in rhythm if material such as this is presented enthusiastically. A life-long love for literature may develop if youngsters are favorably impressed with poetry and prose during the Age of Repetition.

Adult listeners must not lose their appreciation of rhythm's value, but they must make it secondary to content. In Browning's "How They Brought the Good News from Ghent to Aix" the rhythm, figuratively speaking, puts a listener into the saddle:

> I sprang to the stirrup, and Joris, and He;
> I galloped, Dirck galloped, we galloped all three;
> "Good speed!" cried the watch, as the gatebolts undrew;
>
> "Speed!" echoed the wall to us galloping through;
> Behind shut the postern, the lights sank to rest,
> And into the midnight we galloped abreast.

Additionally, an oral reader must give consideration not only to the overall fundamental rhythm of a story-verse, but she must also recognize the value of specific words that contribute vitally to the movement. The duration of given vowel sounds provides the key to action. Observe the effect of prolonging and shortening vowels in the following underlined examples:

> The avalanche smashed and ground down the mountain.
> His fist splattered the outlaw's nose.
> Fluffy, white clouds dotted the azure sky.

Prolongation of vowels would assist action in the first two sentences. Rhythm, however, would be impaired in the third sentence if vowel sounds were lengthened. "Fluffy" sounds fluffier if the vowel is soft and short. Adept word handling enhances the imaginative quality of poetry and makes excursions into the realm of literature more enjoyable for children.

AFTER THE STORY

The type of story and the purpose for which it is told will determine the action a storyteller should take when the tale has concluded. Children should have a brief period at the close of a story to reflect upon it. This will reinforce the story's message. In general, a story with a serious theme should be followed by a longer pause than one with a whimsical mood. The length of reflection will depend upon the level of control enjoyed by the teacher. In some situations, a moment of silence would be the signal for some children to create disorder. Following a period of reflection, a teacher may ask if there are any questions or observations class members might want to make. Discussing a story's implications or having children share personal experiences similar to those in a story provide an excellent means of developing communicative facility.

Having children tell back a story is an excellent means of reinforcing the tale. This may be done by outright recall by various members of the group or the teacher may show pictures from a well-illustrated book and let the pictures remind the children of the story's sequence. Another feedback technique is to give flannel board objects appropriate to a story to members of the group. As the story is retold, the children will apply their objects to the flannel board at the proper moment.

Art work may also follow storytelling. Children may draw, color and cut out silhouette pictures depicting some aspect of the story. These may be assembled into a composite scene from the tale or they may be retained by the children for their own pleasure. The latter course of action is probably preferable if there is danger that less gifted children will come to dislike storytelling because their subsequent artistic efforts to draw or paint do not compare to work done by more talented classmates.

Story acting is another excellent follow-up activity. Details on this form of educational endeavor will be found in Chapter 5.

SUMMARY

This chapter has recommended procedure for the preparation and presentation of stories. The section devoted to story preparation has stressed the importance of maintaining a lively audience interest by presenting a short introduction, a body characterized by action and suspense that moves directly toward a climax and a quick conclusion that follows immediately upon the climax. Story preparation will be facilitated by studying the author's life, associating personal experiences with situations in a story, studying a story's setting, "acting" out its scenes and mastering the meaning of every word, sentence and paragraph. Storytellers are urged to seek out a story's key situations and then prepare cue cards that will facilitate delivery. Use of a tape recorder will assist a teacher to develop appropriate volume, articulation, pronunciation and rate of delivery. This section reminds the reconteur that the story is the primary consideration and the teller is secondary. Storytellers will suggest action, interpret the conversation of various characters, but will not literally act out the parts.

The actual telling of a story must be preceded by physical preparation that insures comfort for children and cuts distractions to a minimum. The teacher must be easily seen and heard during her presentation and she must be capable of adapting to her group as her story unfolds. Stories may be read as well as told. Some materials lend themselves to the former mode of delivery because of their vocabulary or form. Read stories are enhanced when good eye contact is demonstrated by the reader, when rhythm is appropriate to the age level of a group and when a reader is fully identified with an author's work.

Follow-up activity after a story may take the form of tell back, art work of various types and story acting.

"Rapunzel Rapunzel"

FOLLOWUP TO "RAPUNZEL"

Drawn by, Miss Gay Reid, Commodore Bainbridge School, Bainbridge Island, Washington.

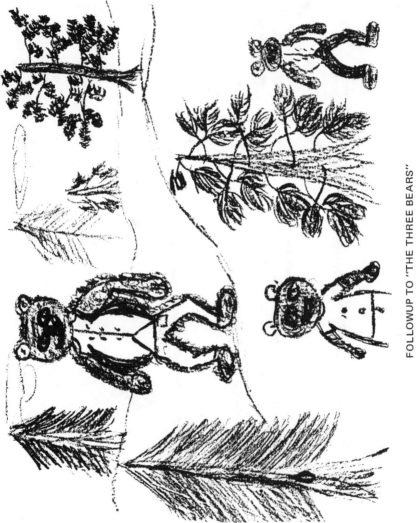

FOLLOWUP TO "THE THREE BEARS"

Drawn by, Miss Rita Rockstad, Commodore Bainbridge School, Bainbridge Island, Washington.

52

FOLLOWUP TO "HANSEL AND GRETEL"

Drawn by, Miss Gay Reid, Commodore Bainbridge School, Bainbridge Island, Washington.

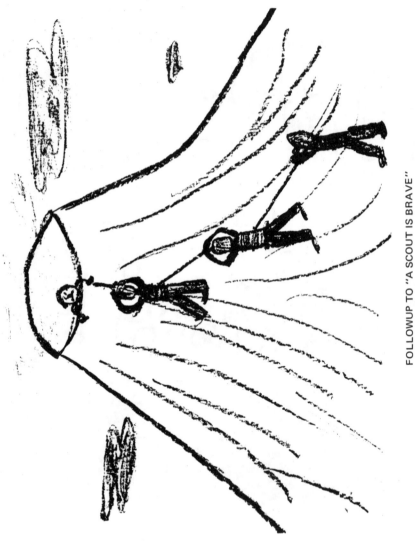

FOLLOWUP TO "A SCOUT IS BRAVE"

Drawn by, Miss Rita Rockstad, Commodore Bainbridge School, Bainbridge Island, Washington.

5

Dramatic Play

What It Is

Dramatic play is characteristic of childhood. Young children imitate the mannerisms and actions of older children and their parents. They pantomime floor sweeping, book reading, car driving, lawn mowing and other activities that fall within their sphere of experience. The whistle or bell-ringing from ice cream vending trucks brings a "toot-toot" or a "ding-dong" from children on the sidewalk. As children grow older, they seek the company of others in dramatic play. The urge to create and imitate finds expression in backyard "dramas" complete with an improvised or imaginary stage and costumes selected from the discarded clothing of their elders. When children creatively reenact a short story or a scene from one, using their own words and actions, it may be said that they are story acting.

Its Values

The values of this activity are many and varied. Inasmuch as story acting does not involve memorized lines, children say what comes naturally. This stimulates their imaginations, emotions and idea development. The feelings of success and adequacy that come from this activity are conducive to self-confidence.

Story acting knows no color lines. Children accept each other regardless of race, creed or color. The play is the thing, and the actors cooperate to make it successful. Social adjustment and unity is a valuable byproduct of this endeavor.

Children soon discover that in order to be appreciated, they must be understood. Speech patterns may improve as performers are motivated to correct defects of pronunciation and articulation.

Story acting permits children to choose the scene they wish to play, the length of time they wish to perform, the number of characters required and the number and kind of "props" to be used. They may evaluate their own effort if they choose and seek to improve it. This activity is a good example of democracy in action. It is a form of self-government in the realm of creative activity.

The value of story acting as pure fun must not be overlooked. The routine that is so characterisitic of classrooms, Sunday School classes, youth meetings and playgrounds can be enlivened by this activity.

Characteristics of a Story for Acting

Stories for acting must be popular with the group and easily understood by them. There should be an abundance of conversation of an uncomplicated nature. For example, stories for acting on the pre-school level should contain such simple conversational sequence as, "Not I," said the duck and "Not I," said the pig. Children who are old enough to read, may be assisted by having a brief sequence of events listed on the chalkboard.

The story must have an abundance of action. The latter, however, must be feasible for dramatizing. A Paul Bunyan tale, though desirable for telling, would fall short as an acted story because the children could not approach the exaggerated nature of the action demanded. Likewise, a tale from the Arabian Nights that required a flying carpet would give difficulty. A dramatized story must be more effective for the child when it is acted than when it is told. If certain aspects of the tale make it impossible to enact satisfactorily, the participants will feel "let down."

Stories for acting should have numerous characters. This permits greater group participation and enables more children to feel the thrill of adequacy that comes from this activity. The teacher should avoid a story such as Dinah Mulock's "The Little Lame Prince" in which one child is alone most of the time. In contrast, "The Bremen Town Musicians," "The Little Rabbit That Wanted Wings" and "The Boy Who Cried Wolf" permit many children to join in the fun.

Stories for acting should also have appropriate emotional appeal and contain worthwhile ideas. The former permits more ready identification with the plot and its characters. The emotional response to an exciting climax may be very satisfying to youngsters. A suitable story will exemplify desirable social conduct and confine itself to a single plot. A compounded plot, replete with digressions, may frustrate and confuse even the most attentive and conscientious child actors.

Getting Started

Occasionally a teacher new to story acting will become impatient with the groping for ideas that may characterize this activity. She may wish to step in to show the group how some action should be handled. This, of course, would destroy an exercise completely. Developing freedom through creativity is the goal . . . the quality of acting is of little concern. Some teachers are also discouraged when a story is acted with little evidence of creativity . . . with children woodenly performing the action. Patience and perseverance will reward teacher and child alike. Perhaps after a dull performance the teacher may casually discuss the personality traits of the story's characters to refresh this information in the children's minds. The next cast to try the scene or story may come up with some delightful innovations. Gradually fear and inhibitions will fade and confidence will take their places.

Pantomime: One of the easiest ways to introduce story acting is through pantomime. This approach is popular with all ages and it is practiced with varying degrees of complexity from nursery school to collegiate players. One form is to have a participant respond to a relatively simple direction. A teacher may ask, "How many of you have eaten watermelon?" The entire group usually becomes involved by raising hands and the teacher then says, "Who would like to show me how to do it?" Another method of handling pantomime is to have the teacher read a story the children understand and have them react to their part in the story. This approach is especially satisfactory for children with very short attention spans even though it does not lend wings to their imagination as much as story acting which is dependent upon the child's ability to recall. Following are exercises that will help children learn to concentrate and also stimulate their imaginations:

1. Sink to earth like a snowflake.
2. Fan yourself on a hot day.
3. Pick a rose and "stick" yourself on a thorn as you do so.
4. Feed your dog, cat, bird, etc.
5. Mail a letter.
6. Read a letter containing good news, bad news, frightening news.
7. Eat a sour pickle, candy, spaghetti.
8. Plant a row of seeds.
9. Hide a treasure.
10. Mistaken identity: you speak to a student you do not know.
11. You have a poor connection as you speak on the telephone.

12. You speak to a long-winded friend on the telephone, and your father wants you to hang up the receiver.
13. Seek and find a seashell on the seashore.
14. You bite into an apple and see a worm hole.
15. Vacuum the rug.
16. Adjust pictures on the wall.
17. Read a love note.
18. Wash dishes.
19. Measure, fry and flip pancakes.
20. Dribble and shoot a basket.
21. Hook a fish, play it and then lose it.
22. Build a house of cards and have it collapse prematurely.
23. Spade a flower bed.
24. Select fruit at a market.
25. Thread a needle and sew fine cloth; then heavy, coarse cloth.
26. Carefully arrange flowers and then angrily shove them off the table.
27. Peel an onion; then a banana.
28. Indicate by your actions that you are confined in a small cell.
29. Kiss your mother; then a boyfriend.
30. Tune in a TV program you loathe . . . then change channels and show pleasure.
31. Follow directions on a cereal box fold-up.
32. Swing a golf club.
33. Put a worm on a fish hook.
34. You are a photographer taking a baby's picture.
35. Put on false eyelashes, contact lens.
36. Walk barefooted on a gravelly stream bottom.
37. Walk as an old man, an inebriate, a flirt.
38. You have confused your date calendar; answer the doorbell as your second boyfriend arrives.
39. Mow heavy, wet grass; then mow a light, thin growth.
40. Shave with a straight-edge razor.
41. You walk alone, without light, on a dark, wooded path.
42. Direct traffic.
43. Comb unruly, snarled hair.
44. You are alone at home at night; you hear a noise and then see a doorknob turn.
45. Attempt to reason with an assailant; then seize a club and drive him away.

Interrogation: After a group has developed ease with pantomime, the teacher may move to story acting. To accomplish this successfully requires more than simply telling a suitable story and then calling for volunteers to act out the parts. A student teacher reported that she had told her class the story of "Goldilocks and the Three Bears" and, after casting it, the children "just sat." These young thespians were new to story acting and needed encouragement and guidance. Story-related interrogation of the children would have assisted this teacher.

Children should be asked questions regarding their story that demand action or creative answers. Questions such as "Was the little bear happy?" should be avoided. A nod, a shake of the head, an indifferent shrug, a grunt, or a chorus answer might be the response to this question. Instead, the group might be asked, "What did the little bear say when he discovered that his chair had been broken?" or "What expression could the little bear have had on his face when he discovered his chair had been broken?" Children will "feed-back" casting requirements if the following-type questions are asked:

"How many children were there in the story?"
"What kind of animals were there in this story?"
"How many animals do we need to act out this story?"
"Why do we need trees, rocks, or a gate for acting this story?"

Interrogation should also bring out the main points or the key situations of a story. In the case of Goldilocks, the teacher might have asked:

"Why did the three bears decide to take a walk?"
"How did Goldilocks get into the house?"
"What did she do first?"
"After tasting porridge, what did she do?"
"After eating the porridge and sitting on the chairs, where did Goldilocks go?"
"Where did the bears find Goldilocks?"
"What did Goldilocks do upon awakening?"

When the group is thoroughly familiar with the story and its characters, it is time to prepare for casting. In the foregoing instance of the children who "just sat" after they had been cast into various roles, there was a need for a "warm up." The group must be given opportunities to identify with actions of the characters. Before attempting to cast any of the roles, the teacher should encourage group members to imitate mannerisms of the characters. As the first step toward overcoming inhibitions and orienting youngsters, she might ask: "How do you think the father bear walked?" Two, three, or ten children might go before the class to demonstrate the lumbering gait of the big bear. By similar means, the walk of the mother and the little bear might be shared. Next the group might be asked, "How do you think the little bear would eat?" After this activity is explored, the teacher might ask the following questions:

"What do you think the mother bear said to the father bear when they took their walk?"
"What do you think the baby bear said?"

These questions should be discussed. Then teams of three children could stroll before the group acting and talking in the manner they imagined the three bears did when they walked through the woods. Through this gradual introduction, the children get the "feel" of the plot and its characters. Most important of all, they begin to lose their fear of trying. A timid child who otherwise would have declined to play-act the part of the father bear might volunteer to do so because demonstrating the animal's walk had given him the confidence to try to play the larger part. Volunteers should also be sought to act the parts of trees, bushes, and large rocks found along the path travelled by the bears. Before casting, children could demonstrate actions such as the following:

"How would a Christmas tree stand?"
"How would an oak tree stand?"
"How would a weeping willow stand?"

A pine tree might be simulated by joining hands over head with elbows bent; oak trees might be represented with outstretched arms in a more horizontal position. Weeping willows might be suggested by limp hands with fingers pointed toward the ground, and the child's chin resting on his chest. The group might also be asked, "What kind of weather did the three bears have on their walk?" If the children respond, "Windy," the teacher could ask, "How do trees act in the wind?" Various class members could come into the acting area and demonstrate the swaying and bending that they believe a certain type tree might do.

When preparing older children for story-acting, questions may be more abstract. For example, fourth graders, orienting to "Cinderella" might be asked:

"How did Cinderella feel when she learned that she could not go to the ball?"
"If you had been there as her friend, what might she have said to you?"
"What might you have said to her?"
"What do you think Cinderella said to the prince as she danced with him?"
"What do you think the prince said to her?"
"How did Cinderella carry her dress?"

If children were being prepared to story act "Androcles and the Lion" they could be asked:

"What did the king say when the lion refused to attack Androcles?"
"If the lion had been able to talk, what would he have said when he recognized Androcles?"
"What did Androcles say to the king when he was given his freedom?"
"If the king had not mentioned freedom for the lion, what do you think Androcles might have said to win freedom for the beast?"

Casting the Story

Ideally, a child who needs play-acting experience would volunteer for the part that would benefit him the most. When introducing story acting to a class, expediency may demand that the most dramatically-capable child, not necessarily the most needful, be placed in key roles until the group orients itself to the process of dramatic play. Since children often clamor to reenact the same story several times, the less gifted child may assume a key position in subsequent performances. This order of selection will give a less talented or introverted youngster the benefit of learning appropriate action by watching others perform. Although imitation is not creative, it is preferred in the case of a slower child because it helps to prevent inappropriate actions which might further stigmatize him before his group. Teachers should be alert for various signals which indicate a child is "volunteering." A shy student, by a nod, a half-smile, or other signs, may be saying, "I am too afraid to raise my hand, but I would like to be in the story." Bashful children might be cast as trees, rocks, signposts, flowers, or birds, until a series of successful experiences emboldens them to try a "talking" role.

Acting the Story

Story acting is *for the children who do the acting,* not an audience. Children act out a story, improvising as their creative spirit moves them. *The child's willingness to try to develop his artistic potential creatively, not his accuracy as to content, is the important consideration.* This premise was illustrated when one group of children, acting out the story of the three bears, happened upon a delightful and startling conclusion. The mother bear spontaneously invited the intruder, Goldilocks, to stay for dinner. Goldilocks accepted and they became friends!

Most story dramatizing is done in a classroom with imaginary props. Once again, the teacher will motivate and indirectly guide the children by asking questions:

"What can we use to show where the three bears' house is?"
"What can we use for the three bowls that hold the bears' porridge?"
"Is there anything here that we can use for the bears' beds?"

Suddenly a corner of the classroom may become the bears' house with two chairs serving as the doorway. Books become bowls of porridge. One bench, which mysteriously causes a different response every time a child rests on it, serves as three beds. As long as a teacher-asking, children-telling relationship is maintained, the story-acting situation will remain creative.

Dramatization of stories can be introduced more smoothly if the material acted is not too comprehensive in scope. The children could start with a short scene or only part of one. A beginning effort could be the hot porridge action followed by the decision to go for a walk. This first presentation would terminate at the point where the bears return to their home. Although a story may be well-known to children, the idea of acting it is usually new. Portraying a small portion that may be completed in one session gives the actors and the observers as well a feeling of fulfillment. Their familiarity with a story helps a group pick up the plot easily in the future, thereby offsetting the loss in continuity which results when the clock terminates dramatization.

Teachers should not attempt to introduce a complete story and act it in the same session. Several sessions normally are required to prepare children for the moment when they volunteer to participate in the presentation of an entire scene or story. During the periods of preparation and acting, the children should be encouraged to forget themselves and try to feel as if they are a bear, tree, rock, or whatever the scenes require. A child actor should not be interrupted as long as he stays in character. A child cannot become creative by being criticized. However, if he winks or makes faces at classmates in the audience, exaggerates his role beyond reason, or otherwise destroys illusion for others who act and observe, he should be quietly replaced without reprimand. He will undoubtedly know why corrective action was necessary and his next attempt will probably be characterized by better judgment.

Listening to the Story

Children engaged in story acting have a right to perform without disturbance from non-participating members of the class. Motivating the latter to listen critically during dramatic activity will lessen chances of disruption. Chapter 8, "Listening" will assist the development of listening habits. The following specific suggestions should prove helpful for story acting:

One or more children may be assigned to each participant for the purpose of listing helpful suggestions that can be shared after the story or scene has been acted. All listeners will be expected to observe all actors, but special attention should be given to assigned buddies by non-acting class members.

Another helpful device is to double or triple cast a scene. This intensifies the interest of the observers in the roles they are going to play.

Children are usually happy to listen if they have developed standards of appreciation. The following questions relating to story acting will sharpen their listening ability:

SPEECH

"Were voices loud enough?" "Could you hear without effort?"
"Were all words clearly pronounced?" "How did you know?"
"Could you hear clearly when the actor's back was turned?" "How did he make himself heard under these conditions?"
"If you could not hear him, how can we help him?"

IDENTIFICATION WITH ROLE

"Did you forget that you knew the boys and girls and feel that they were the characters in the story?" "Why?"

"Did the actors' expressions look the way you think the real characters in the story might have?"

"Did the actor's voices sound as if they meant what they said?"

"Were they sad or happy when the characters were sad or happy?" "How did they show it?"

PLOT

"Was the purpose of the scene or story clear to you?" "How?"

"What was the most important point in the scene?"

"Did you like the story better when it was told or acted?" "Why?"

"Were you satisfied with the ending of the story?" "Why?"

CAST RELATIONS

"Did the characters seem to belong together?" "How did they show this?"

"Did the father and mother bear act as parents should toward each other?" "How did you know?"

"Was the baby bear obedient to his parents?" "How did he show it?"

"Do you think Goldilocks was friendly?" "Did she have good manners?"

Good listening habits will be encouraged if children are convinced that their teacher respects their opinions. If they feel that their suggestions have helped to make the group's effort a successful experience, they will listen more attentively in the future. Formulating constructive judgments will assist them to develop a positive attitude toward story acting.

Evaluation

After each presentation it will prove educationally worthwhile to discuss the dramatization done by the cast. This period must be one of encouragement, not discouragement. The following suggestions have proved helpful when evaluating:

Praise should characterize the opening remarks of an evaluation. *Nothing succeeds like success.* Minor roles could be acknowledged by such remarks as, "Good work, Jackie! You rolled yourself into a ball and appeared to be a rock." "Class, did you notice how gracefully the trees waved in the breeze? We could almost feel that soft summer wind." "The father bear certainly became fierce when he discovered that someone had entered his house without permission! That is the way to act, father bear!" Referring to the name of the character rather than the actor's name is preferred when praising or criticizing "talking parts."

Following a period of tempered, deserved praise, most children will profit from tactful, constructive criticism. Cast members will indulge in self-evaluation when their leader asks, "What could the actors do to be heard more easily?" "Did any parts of the story confuse you?" "Why?" "Was the mother bear tender to her little bear?" "What would you say to the little bear to make it stop crying when it found its broken chair?" "Did you get excited when the bears approached the house?" "Why?" "Did the actors seem excited when the climax was reached?" "How did you know?"

Kindergartners and first graders generally can do little more than manufacture enough lines to keep a story moving. Evaluation of the efforts of these little ones should be limited to praise by other class members. The teacher may ask, "Boys and girls, what did this group do well?" or "Which part of this story did you especially like?" These comments could be followed by a few constructive criticisms by the teacher. From the second grade on, dramatization should begin to reflect the emotional reactions of the characters. This ability is concomitant with the group's mental age. Joy, fear, disappointment and the like, should begin to become evident through situations which demand these reactions. The more mature the group, the more searching the constructive criticism may become.

The teacher must be prepared to "cushion" remarks made by class members if suggestions become too pointed. For example, a non-participant may say, "I thought Goldilocks was bum when the bears found her. She didn't get scared." The teacher might soften this criticism by saying, "Goldilocks might have acted more frightened but did you notice how quickly she leaped from the bed and ran away? That is how a frightened girl would act." Here the teacher agrees with the critic and yet leaves Goldilocks with a feeling of accomplishment. The evaluation by a group provides an excellent opportunity for creative play which can grow out of the criticism. A child might say, "I don't think Goldilocks acted as if the porridge were too hot when she tried to sip it." The teacher might reply, "Mary will you show us how you think Goldilocks might have acted?" A problem is only directed back to the proposer when the teacher is certain that the child is aggressive enough to try. If a shy child thinks she will be asked to demonstrate the sampling of porridge when she justifiably disagrees with the way it was done, she will not participate in criticism. When a shy child makes the aforementioned comment, the teacher should turn to the class and ask, "Would someone like to taste the hot porridge for us?" She might also turn to the child who played Goldilocks and say, "Goldilocks, would you like to try the porridge again?" The joy of accomplishment leaves a child's heart when derogatory comments go unchallenged by a teacher or when too much constructive criticism, however justified, is heaped upon the participant. A teacher should *never permit too much criticism of a child or a cast.*

ROLE PLAYING

What It Is

Role playing is the spontaneous, unrehearsed acting out of a problem situation which involves human relations. In the latter respect it differs from some forms of creative dramatics which cast children into "playing" trees, rocks, gates, bridges, etc. In role playing, the children's only cues to action are their knowledge of a situation which has been described by the teacher. The importance of spontaneity in this activity should be underlined. In real life, children do not have time for studied responses to situations which arise. If they are permitted to study a problem at great length before role playing, they might be prone to react as they think their teacher or parent want them to react rather than responding frankly and honestly.

Its Values

Role playing may give classrooms a new sense of relevancy by introducing real problems that are frequently confronted in the school and on the playground, in the home and in the community generally.

Participants receive experience and training in problem solving in a very practical sense. Not only does the child have a chance to discuss a problem and "act out" its solution, but he is given an opportunity to evaluate his solution in the light of others that may be presented.

Participants are prone to develop tolerance for other person's feelings and they also discover that there are at least two sides to every problem.

Participants may be assisted to develop personalities that will not require "whipping boys" for the venting of hostility.

Participants will learn, as they explore pertinent dilemma situations, that they are not alone with their problems.

How To Do It

A teacher or group leader begins by reading or extemporaneously relating a story which has a conflict situation typical to the age of the children. If role playing is to be a successful experience, the problem presented must seem important to the group. The narrator terminates the story when its dilemma is reached and says to her listeners, "What would you do in a situation like this, boys and girls?" If the story were well told, if the children become emotionally involved with the characters in the story, the teacher will receive an avalanche of suggestions and answers to her question. After briefly discussing the problem the teacher will ask for volunteers to act the various parts. The same dilemma may be role played two or three times. Situations may involve from two to five or six players.

Before the acting begins, the teacher requests the listeners to avoid overt responses such as clapping, laughing or jeering because it may destroy the player's illusion. Ideally, the actors would be unaware of the audience. If the teacher casts other groups to play the same scene before the first group acts, listening on the part of the class may be more intent. Before acting begins, the players must be reassured that anything they may do in the course of characterization will not be held against them. If a child believes his character demands mean, nasty action, then so be it. They must not be criticized for errors, mispronunciations or other deviations from generally accepted classroom behavior. The teacher should tactfully avoid type-casting. A child should not play his own life's role. The acting should revolve around a problem . . . not an individual.

The scene is enacted without props, staging, lighting or any effort to costume. This is informal drama and the emphasis is on *content* and not the acting. The presentation may be short or extended depending upon the actors' reaction. They might reach a solution or conclude at a point where they feel more information is needed. When role playing, there is no applause for finding a solution or penalty for failure to do so.

Following the presentation, the group should evaluate the results. Portions may be replayed, not to improve acting, but to clarify the ideas expressed. The teacher could guide the evaluation with questions such as the following: Will the solution presented eliminate or modify the causes of the problem? Will the solution eliminate or minimize the bad effects created by the problem? If the solution will solve one problem, will it cause others that are equally undesirable? Children may be led to find a composite solution if a single suggestion is not satisfactory. After the evaluation, another cast could role play the same problem or the original group could perform again in an effort to eliminate problem solving errors revealed during the evaluation. Role playing should be temporarily discontinued if children lose their enthusiasm. If creativity diminishes, pleasure will wane too. Only if motivation is kept high, will role playing lend enchantment to education.

Role playing may have a strong emotional impact on participants and listeners alike. Ministers, youth leaders and classroom teachers have been criticized for conducting role playing activity on the grounds that they may do more harm than good. Those who make this charge must understand that teachers, for example, are compelled to face emotional problems daily, with or without the aid of role playing. Critical handling of a miscreant by an unsympathetic principal or teacher does not offer the opportunity for tension reduction, for replacement of guilt feelings by assurance that may come from role playing, however imperfectly handled. Teachers may find comfort too in the realization that role playing has built-in safeguards; if a group's discussion becomes too threatening, if it strikes too many "nerves" the group will withdraw and the session comes to an end. It is the responsibility of all who work with youth to acquire sufficient training in speech and psychology to detect a child who needs special assistance and refer him to an appropriate staff specialist.

Situations for Exploration

Ages 5—8: Learning to share toys

The problem: Most of the children line up to use the slide. Tommy, the biggest boy in the group, pushes the others aside and takes another turn ahead of his friends. What can be done to help Tommy?

Ages 9—11: Learning to be honest

The problem: Johnny's Sunday school teacher urged her children to do good things for people during the week. On Sunday she asked her pupils to stand, one by one, and share the good things they had done for their friends and neighbors and pets during the past week. Johnny listened to all of the reports of his friends. When his turn came, he too stood and recited a list of good deeds . . . none of which he had done. The more he thought of this dishonest act, the more troubled he became. Should he tell his teacher? His father would punish him. His friends would dislike him for lying. What should Johnny do?

Ages 12—14: Choosing desirable friends

The problem: Paul's family owned a fast ski boat that he became adept at operating. Paul was new in his school and had few friends. Dick, Jim and Jack, all members of the football team and popular on campus, were happy to go skiing with Paul but they never volunteered to defray gasoline costs or help clean up the boat after a day's outing. Tim, a quiet boy in the neighborhood and one who did not make friends easily, also enjoyed boating with Paul and he was willing to pay his share of the expenses. He also remained at the dock at the end of the day until everything was "Bristol fashion." One day Paul told his friends that he had to pull the boat from the water and clean off the barnacles. The clean-up party was set for Saturday. Only Tim showed up to help. The other boys claimed they had forgotten. Should Paul invite them again?

Ages 15—18: Learning the rules of acceptable conduct

The problem: Mary was alone in the girls' restroom combing her hair. Her purse was on a table in back of her. A group of girls came into the room and formed a tight circle near the table. Mary glanced at the girls as they entered and recognized some who had questionable reputations. When she turned to replace her comb in her purse, the latter was gone. Mary was both angered and frightened. The week before another girl had been attacked and slashed with razor blades by this group. Should she accuse them of stealing her purse? Should she tell the school counselor and risk being attacked? Should she tell her parents, realizing that they would worry about her? Should she just forget the whole thing? What would you do?

Additional Problem Situations for Role Playing and Discussion

1. Jeff returns from a Boy Scout hike to discover that his father has been hospitalized following an accident. Lacking funds to hire a special nurse, his mother must stay with his father at the hospital. Jeff doesn't mind being alone on their fruit ranch, but he is worried about a bumper apple crop that must be harvested within the next seven days. His neighbors are sympathetic, but they are faced with harvesting too. What would you do if you were Jeff? His neighbors? The members of his scout troup? His mother?
2. Sue finds a purse containing money and identification on her way to school.
3. You have been denied membership in an organization in which all the "in" students belong.
4. You have difficulty getting dances at school functions because of your skin color.
5. Bill "borrows" money from the family food fund and does not return it. His parents miss the money but blame it on Bill's younger brother.
6. Your history class is studying World War II. How does it feel to be a Japanese-American sent to an internment camp?
·7. Jack catches a winning touchdown pass out of bounds but is not detected by the referee. He knew he was out of bounds but went on to score.
8. Your school is having trouble with older boys who run in the halls when classes are changing. Last week a girl was knocked down and injured.
9. Tom's mother died and his father married a lady who had a son Tom's age. Tom is expected to do the yard work and even scrub the kitchen floor, but the other boy does very little. Tom's father doesn't seem to care about this injustice.
10. Jane was taking tickets at the school play and was told by the principal to admit only ticket holders as the function was a sell out. Two couples, friends of Jane, bustled in, thrust three tickets and cash for another in her hand and kept on walking in spite of her protests. Jane was afraid to tell the principal for fear he would think she was weak. A seating problem did not develop, but Jane did not want the money. What should she do?
11. Luke, a Jewish first grader, is abused by his classmates. Sand is thrown at him and he is called a "kike." Third graders have chased him and beaten him on the way home after school. His mother has started to meet him after school, but she must leave work to do so. Luke does not have a father.

SUMMARY

This chapter has explored story acting and role playing as creative activity growing out of story telling. Although there is some overlapping in these two forms of dramatic play, role playing is dominantly involved with human relations. Both are spontaneous, unrehearsed activities which are indirectly guided by a group leader or teacher. Both activities are conducive to social adjustment, speech improvement, more enjoyable learning, stimulation of imagination and leadership development.

6

The Child
as Storyteller

Each of the preceding chapters has dealt with the teacher as the storyteller. Several of the early authors in the storytelling field have been adamant in their pronouncements that stories should be told *to* children *by* adults. They reasoned that, since children's literature was written by mature persons, it should be interpreted by mature persons. They also expressed the belief that (a) children are incapable of portraying a wide range of emotions, (b) children fail to comprehend the communicative aspects required of the situation and (c) children are too self-centered to project the meaning the author wished to convey. Perhaps these early authors had in mind an occasional audience of children gathered in an auditorium to hear a storyteller, perhaps a Saturday story hour at a library, or possibly an activity in a municipal recreation program. They could hardly anticipate the dynamic impact that today's classroom teachers are exerting on their pupils' interest in the oral communication of literature. The publishing industry is assisting to stimulate interest in children's literature by its release of folk and fairy tales and other children's classics at nominal prices. Many youngsters come to school today laden with their favorite story books. Education specialists have placed considerable value on group-mindedness and procedures for inculcating the ideals of unselfish behavior. Under the prevailing philosophy, a teacher is hesitant to discourage children from bringing their favorite books to school. However, if she attempted to tell or to read all of the stories brought into her classroom by her pupils, little else would be accomplished in the school day. One solution is to have children tell their favorite stories.

When Children Should Participate

A teacher is the model for storytelling effectiveness and she should tell the majority of the stories. At the beginning of the school year, she

69

should spend several weeks weaving stories into her daily teaching before turning over the role to children. This is necessary in spite of the fact that children are more likely to bring stories to school after summer vacation than at any other time during the school year. The following principles should provide some guidance for the teacher:

1. The child should be allowed to tell a story when he feels he wants to do so, not on a set assignment schedule. Real sharing, in the storytelling sense, grows out of a desire to communicate, not out of the compulsion that of necessity must characterize most classroom assignments.
2. No child or group should be permitted to dominate a story-sharing period. Every pupil should have an opportunity to tell a story before any member of the group is allowed to tell a second time.
3. If it appears that many children are reluctant to enter into storytelling activity, the teacher should defer child-told stories for several weeks. When story-sharing is resumed, children who did not participate in earlier sessions should be encouraged to be among the first to share.

Children are usually eager to tell stories in advance of Halloween, Thanksgiving and Christmas. These three occasions seem to have more immediate meaning to children than most other holidays of the school year. Perhaps this is due in part to the presence of stories in increasing numbers which are available in home, school and public libraries. Commercial advertising and home observances of these holidays also enhance their importance. Rapport between a student audience and a student storyteller is more likely to be evidenced for a story told just prior to one of these days. This is a result of group anticipation of the approaching occasion. In order to realize maximum participation in story sharing during these holidays, a teacher may find it advisable to discuss all three dates early in October. During this discussion she should ask which students would like to share a Halloween story, which would prefer to tell a story about Thanksgiving, and which would like to tell a Christmas story. Logically, she will explain that, because time is limited, no child will be permitted to tell a story for more than one occasion.

Children in some fifth and sixth grades have been trained to tell stories to kindergarten-primary age groups! Students who volunteered for training for this activity were given an opportunity to tell their stories during lunch periods. The result of this endeavor was improved speaking ability, a sharpened interest in literature and reading and finally, more children were exposed to good stories in spite of an overtaxed library facility. Many other opportunities for child-storytelling may be made available. Children should be encouraged to recount tales before campfires sponsored by both organization and family groups. When fires blaze in hearths on cold winter evenings, both parents and children may share stories. Halloween parties may be enlivened by child-told stories.

The latter are being employed with increasing frequency in Sunday school lessons. One church group has organized some of its youngsters into a story telling club which visits shut-ins and bedridden children. Classroom teachers may make units on Mexico, Japan, the American Indian and other social studies more interesting by encouraging students to prepare and share stories about these lands and people. Permitting children to tell stories will enable them to participate more intimately in church, school, home and organization activities.

THE CHILD AND THE STORY

Because storytelling by a child has educational value for him in the various facets of the communicative process, a teacher should point out the elements which contribute to effective oral expression. An involved explanation is neither necessary nor desirable, but the following general principles should be discussed with the children (a) *Story Selection.* Everyone in the class should enjoy the story selected by the storyteller. It should appeal to both boys and girls. It should deal with persons other than the storyteller himself, his family, or his pets. It should be a story which the storyteller has heard or read, one he likes, and one which he has rehearsed many times. (b) *Time Limits.* Most children are willing to become storytellers. Too often their train of thought is sidetracked midway through the story. Digressions from the theme creep in, and the child ends up monopolizing the entire period. As one teacher so aptly put it, "Getting children started with storytelling is no problem; what I want to know is how to stop them." A five minute time limit is ample for nearly every child-told story. This will enable more children to participate and, if enforced, will produce better story preparation. A member of the class may be designated as timekeeper and this duty rotated among the group from day to day. The timekeeper should raise his hand at the end of five minutes, and stand at the end of six minutes. The five minute signal would indicate that a one minute "grace period" remains in which the story must be concluded. The time limit should be clearly stated by the teacher before beginning any child-told stories. She might demonstrate this by designating a student timekeeper and then proceeding with a story of her own. (c) *Posture.* A child should stand when telling a story. This facilitates delivery and insures easy viewing of the narrator by the audience. (d) *Expression.* Usually, children are less inhibited than adults. Subconsciously, they enjoy identification with all of the characters in a story. Gestures should be encouraged, vocal variety praised, and mood-conveying changes in facial expression complimented. (e) *Audibility.* In defiance of an old axiom, in a child-told story, children should be both seen and heard. A teacher may wish to sit in the rear of the room and signal the storyteller if he is inaudible. The usual sign is simply a raised hand. A child should be informed in advance of the signal to be used. (f) *Rate.* The rapid rate at which many children speak can prove a serious obstacle to effective storytelling. The child must be assisted to realize that his story is new to the class and that it must be delivered slowly enough for everyone to follow the plot. Children should be encouraged to let the action in the story determine their rate of utterance. Identification with the characters and the details of the story is necessary to effect this. If the child has difficulty with the latter, it might be necessary to have him volitionally reduce his speed. This may be accomplished by having the teacher sit at the rear of the room and hand signal. The radio-television director's signal is a taffy-pulling gesture with both hands. This action intrigues most children. (g) *Visual Aids.* When child-told stories are first initiated, it is entirely in order for children to use illustated stories, and to show pictures simultaneously with the action of the tale. They should be advised, however, to bring stories with pictures which are large enough to be seen by the entire class. Examples of appropriate sized pictures should be exhibited. When using a story with pictures, the illustrations should be held high enough for all to see, and they should be shown long enough to provide an adequate impression of a scene or character. As the children become accustomed to their role as storytellers, it is advisable for the teacher to ask them to tell a story without using visual aids. This should not be an actual requirement, for some youngsters may never be able to present a story without the support of a picture. Young storytellers may be motivated in this direction by challenging them to use such vivid descriptions and such vital expression in their voice and gestures that everyone can be made to see the scene or character. (h) *Teacher Assistance.* Frequently some children will forget the plot at some point or perhaps omit an important character. The teacher may assist the child if she knows in advance which stories are going to be told. She may wish to encourage her students to give her the book just prior to the child's presentation in order that she may act as prompter. If a child should forget, become exceedingly nervous, or fail to respond to prompting the teacher may help him "save face" by saying, "Tommy, you have certainly aroused our interest in your story. Would you read the rest of it?" The teacher might offer further help by asking members of the class how they thought the story concluded. If this does not stimulate the memory of the storyteller, she could ask him to tell the story again on the following day.

CRITICISM OF THE CHILD-TOLD STORY

While lasting benefits in oral communication skills may result from the child-told story, it is usually not a curricular subject and never a discipline. Criticism of student presentations needs to be handled diplomatically. A shy child should be guided gently toward the development of confidence before his classmates. The exhibitionist needs kindly advice to show him how to fit his expressive nature into a structured situation in which sharing is the goal. Assuming that only two or three children can present their stories in a given day, the teacher may easily jot down her observations on each presentation. As soon after the story hour as possible, she may speak with each child participant individually. He should be praised for that which was commendable about his performance and then given a tactful suggestion or two which will help him tell his next story. Sharing is one of the major goals in elementary education and it is recommended that the entire class join in evaluation. The teacher must structure the evaluation to conform with the goals the group is currently striving to attain. For example, prior to the story the children might be told, "The tale Jack is about to tell has interesting characters. Let us see if we would want them for friends." Following the story, the group may discuss the level of characterization reached by Jack. In a like manner, children may be prepared to discuss the description of scenes, the sequence of action, plot development, word choice and other aspects of story development.

PARTICIPATION STORIES

Stories of this type may be told by either teacher or child. They depend on the active participation of all class members for their effectiveness. Student participation follows an established cue line in the story and may take the form of bodily activity, words or nonsense syllables. Participation stories are strictly for fun. Indeed, teenagers and adults seem to enjoy them as much as children. In general, participation stories should be short and uncomplicated. Usually a maximum of eight different cues can be remembered by the middle and upper grade children, and eight different participation responses appear to be the limit of memory for this age group. A good participation story can be told (played) many times before the same group during the school year. The initial success of a participation story depends upon the clarity of the cues and the action called for. Both of these are the responsibility of the storyteller and they must be thoroughly explained before beginning the story. It is advisable to rehearse the audience before beginning the actual story. The action desired for each cue must be clearly explained. For example, a storyteller might say, "When you hear the word 'tiger', make a grrr sound. Let us all make the grrr sound now for practice." After all cues for action have been explained, the teacher may double back and ask, "When I say the word 'tiger', what is the sound you are to make?" Rehearsal of this kind will make the participation story more pleasurable for all concerned.

CHOOSING PARTICIPATION STORIES

Many teachers have found it expedient and effective to adapt familiar folk tales to participation story form. If a teacher elects to do this (with "The Three Billy Goats Gruff," "The Three Bears," "The Gingerbread Boy" or any other well-known story), she should try to put the action on vocal participation at the ends of sentence. Otherwise, the story becomes almost unrecognizable because of imposed interjections. Following are versions of three stories which have met with enthusiastic response in the classroom, around the campfire and on playgrounds. A host of similar stories abound, many of which are familiar to a reader.

ONE WINTER NIGHT
Cues

Wind	— Ho-o-o-o	Grandfather's Clock	— Click Tongue
Cat	— Meow-ooo	Horse	— Neigh
Dog	— Arf-arf-arf	Cow	— Moo-oo
Baby	— Cry	Loud Noise	— Yell
Asleep	— Snore	Rain	— Hands Slapping on Knees

It was a stormy winter night. The *wind* whistled down the chimney of the little farm house, and the *rain* beat against the windows. Inside, the family sat around the fireplace. The *cat* and the *dog* played on the hearth, mother held the *baby* in her lap, and above the sound of the *wind* and *rain* could be heard the ticking of the old *grandfather's clock*.

Out in the barn the *horse* and the *cow* grew restless as the *wind* blew *harder*, and *harder* and *harder*. Hearing a *loud noise*, the man and his *dog*, leaving the warm fireside to the *cat* and the *baby*, hurried outside to the barn to see what the *loud noise* could be. The wind had only blown the barn door open and the *horse* and the *cow* were safe, so the man and his *dog* returned to the warm fire, where the *baby* and the *cat* were sound *asleep*.

The *rain* and the *wind* grew *softer*, and *softer* and *softer*, and above all could be heard the ticking of the old *grandfather's clock*.

BRAVE LITTLE INDIAN
Cues

Brave Little Indian — Put one hand to the back of your head with fingers showing above the head.
Indian walks on the road — Slap one knee, then the other.
Indian walks on the bridge — Slap chest with fists.
Indian swims — Rub hands together, being careful not to slap them.
(On return trip, speed up the tempo)

Once upon a time there was a "Brave Little Indian Boy" (sign) who lived in a village with many other "Brave Little Indian Boys" (sign). One day the "Brave Little Indian Boy" said to the others, "I'm going out to find a big brown bear." And all the other "Brave Little Indian Boys" said, "UGH."

So the "Brave Little Indian Boy" started to walk, walk, walk, walk, (sign) until he came to a bridge. Then he began to walk, walk, walk, walk, walk, walk, (sign) until he got to the other side. Then he began to walk, walk, walk, walk, walk, walk, walk, walk, (sign) until he came to a river. Then he began to swim, swim, swim, swim, swim, swim, swim, swim, (sign) until he got to the other side. Suddenly, he stopped. The "Brave Little Indian Boy" (sign) saw a big, brown bear. He turned around and started to run, run, run, run, run, run, run, run. (sign) When he came to river, he began to swim, swim, swim, swim, swim, swim, swim, swim. (sign) When he reached the other side, he began to run, run, run, run, run, run, run, run (sign) until he came right up to the village. And he said to all the other "Brave Little Indian Boys" (sign), "I saw a BIG BROWN BEAR." And all the other "Brave Little Indian Boys" (sign) said, "UGH."

HERE WE GO ON A LION HUNT

(This version of "The Lion Hunt" is the basic story. Use your own words. The plan is, that one person sits before the group, tells the story, and leads out the action.)

Once upon a time, in an African village, there was a brave Chief whose name O-o-o-o-o-o! (Speak the Chief's name in a low tone, BEATING CHEST AT THE SAME TIME.) He had a devoted wife whose name was Ah-h-h-h-h-h! (Speak the wife's name in a high tone, BEATING CHEST AT THE SAME TIME WITH BOTH FISTS.)

Now it happened that a lion had been stealing the sheep, belonging to the people of the village. Somebody had to be chosen to hunt the lion. Who do you think it was? Well, it was O-o-o-o-o-o.

The villagers gathered outside the hut, and when their chief came out, there arose a great hubbub. (FOR HUBBUB, ALL FEMALE VOICES CHANT "SODDA WATTA BOTTL," OVER AND OVER AGAIN IN A HIGH VOICE WHILE MALES SAY SLOWLY AND RHYTHMICALLY IN LOW VOICE, "RHUBARB RHUBARB.") After the people had said fond good-byes to their chief, they opened the gate (PUT HANDS TOGETHER, THEN STRETCH THEM WIDELY) and closed it behind him. (CLAP HANDS BACK TOGETHER.)

It was a beautiful day. O-o-o-o-o-o walked along (TO REPRESENT WALKING, SLAP LEFT THIGH WITH LEFT HAND, THEN RIGHT THIGH WITH RIGHT HAND, ETC., IN SLOW WALKING RHYTHM.) He looked to the right of him (DO SO) and looked to the left of him (DO SO) and sniffed the spring air (SNIFF) but there was no lion around.

So he continued to walk along with ease. (WALK) Before long he came to a covered bridge, but he didn't stop. (FOR COVERED BRIDGE SOUND: THUMP CHEST WITH RIGHT FIST THEN LEFT FIST, ALTER-NATELY, IN SAME RHYTHM AS WALKING.) He walked right on and still no lion.

Before long he came to a wide creek. He stopped. (STOP) (POINT) Crocodiles! (PUT BASE OF PALMS TOGETHER, SNAP FINGERS TO-GETHER SEVERAL TIMES TO IMITATE CROCODILES.) He walked backwards to get a good running start (DO SO) and ran (FASTER MO-TIONS THAN WALKING) right up to the bank. (STOP) He couldn't make it. So he backed up again. (BACK UP AGAIN) Then he ran just as fast as he could to the bank. (RUN UP AGAIN) He stopped. He couldn't make it. He backed up the third time. "This time I'm going to make it if I have to swim," he said. So he ran up to the creek, dived in and swam (DO IT WILDLY) to the other side. There he shook himself off (DO SO) and started to look out for the ferocious lion. He looked to the right of him (DO SO) and to the left of him (DO SO) and sniffed the sweet spring air, (DO SO) but he saw no lion.

He even climbed a tree (DO SO) and looked out (DO SO) but saw no lion. So he came down. Now he walked up the side of a tall hill (WALK SLOWER, PANT) and then through the tall grass to the mouth of a cave. (SWISH HANDS TOGETHER FOR TALL GRASS) He looked in cautiously, first to the left of him (DO SO). No lion! Then to the right of him (DO SO). No lion! Then he looked straight ahead. G-R-R-R-R-R-R-! LION!

O-o-o-o-o-o started back to the village as fast as he could go . . . through the tall grass, down the hill, around the tree, across the creek through the covered bridge. The tribesmen made a terrific hubbub when they saw he was coming back. Quickly they opened the gate, let him in, closed it, and the lion was running so fast that he hit his neck on the gate, broke it, and died. Everybody, little and big, lived happily ever after.

(ON THIS LAST PARAGRAPH REPEAT ALL THE ACTIONS OF THE STORY)

WORD SCRAMBLE

Another variation of the participation story is the word scramble. This delightful means of stimulating thinking consists of taking the following list of words (or a list of a teacher's own choosing, or a list of words volunteered by a group of children), dividing the class into groups of six or eight children, and instructing each group to prepare a story incorporating the words on the list:

sword	boy	mountain	moonlight	box
ransom	TV	space ship	shoes	chair
witch	care	lungs	shipwreck	pail
path	pirate	snow	girl	tree
beautiful	pen	sniff	candle	haystack
cheese	kiss	tongue	spinach	toe

SUMMARY

This chapter hopes to encourage storytelling by children. Youngsters usually begin to tell stories to their classmates in the early grades and hopefully, continue for the rest of their lives. This activity should always be fun and not a mandatory assignment. Sharing should grow out of a desire to communicate. Stories told by children should have a time limitation and be interesting not only to the narrator but to his classmates as well. Teachers should assist children who forget their stories and criticism should be tactful, constructive and conducted privately. Every effort should be made to give a child feelings of adequacy after he has told a story. This activity may increase a child's interest in good literature.

7

Listening

LISTENING HABITS

The American people, generally, have been called poor listeners. Many persons turn on the radio and simultaneously read a book. All too often, college students find a lecture period the ideal time to prepare an assignment for the next class. The advertising men fill their radio and television copy with exaggerated claims in a frantic attempt to capture the attention of consumers. Indeed, this generation has grown accustomed to a noisome existence. This existence is made tolerable, however, by ignoring a certain amount of speech, music, advertising claims and the irritating cacophony of thousands of automobiles seemingly headed in the same direction at the same time.

Added to the problem of noise are the tensions, the pressures and the deadlines which go hand-in-hand with a highly competitive urban culture. Small wonder that, as audiences, people are easily distracted; that they are impatient for the speaker to "get to his point"; that to many of them, creative and constructive listening is a time-consuming luxury they can no longer afford.

What are the implications of these poor listening habits for children? *Basically, the child is a mediocre listener.* He is self-centered and his attention span is brief. This has been true through centuries and in all cultures which possess recorded histories. Until the last generation or two in this country, however, adults have been models of listening behavior for their children. Young and old alike trooped into the Chatauqua grounds, sat on hard benches in the heat of summer, and listened to the artists and lecturers of yesteryear. Of course Robert G. Ingersoll and William Jennings Bryan were beyond the comprehension of pre-adolescents, and the social implications of *Uncle Tom's Cabin* were lost to children. Notwithstanding, under the adult listening code of sixty years ago, the youngsters were silent. Watching the reaction of parents and older brothers and sisters, these children became aware that adults found satisfaction in paying attention.

Sixty years ago, churchgoers sat as a family. Children sat through Sunday school *and* through church. It would be ridiculous to claim that the behavior of all children was exemplary. Some infants cried, some toddlers wiggled and some juniors became fidgety. In spite of these obstacles to a reverent mood, every child could observe about him the respect and response of adults to the sermon.

Chautauqua has been replaced by the ubiquitous, uncritical and half-listened to television set. A child now observes his adult models talking to each other as they watch *their* programs and leaving him alone in the room during *his* programs. Few children under the age of twelve can be seen these days sitting in the pews of urban churches. Shuttled off to their peer groups while the regular worship service is being held in the sanctuary, they can no longer learn first-hand the meaning of reverential listening. Thus it is that the listening habits of late twentieth century American children are primarily conditioned by the adult community. The pressures and tensions which afflict grownups are reflected in their children.

WHY CHILDREN DO NOT LISTEN

A child who is a poor listener frequently has this habit well-established before he enters a classroom. If parents greet their child's efforts to speak with, "Not now, Junior, can't you see I'm busy," or "Come back after this program is over," or "Please be quiet . . . can't you do anything but ask questions?" etc., the rejected juvenile communicator may learn to look upon negativism as a normal response as he attempts to communicate orally. Parents who lack the patience or stamina to work sympathetically with their child as he struggles for the skill to express his feelings may find themselves rewarded with inattention. They will hear themselves saying, "Can't you get anything right?" "I've told you six times to close the door!" "Is there something wrong with your ears?" In the last instance the parent might have inadvertently asked an intelligent question. A child's auditory perception must be normal if he is expected to develop adequate listening behavior. Assuming that a child's hearing is normal, the fact remains that he, not his parents or later his teacher, is the controller of the learning process. He possesses the power to "turn off his ears" when he becomes exhausted or loses interest. It has been indicated that listening is a reciprocal process between a sender and a receiver. In order to learn to listen, a child must have an attentive listener who is genuinely interested. Kindergarten teachers report that their good listeners usually have a mother or someone else who cares for them, who will listen sympathetically and carefully when they wish to speak! The climate for learning established by a classroom teacher has a significant effect on the learning process. Even though a teacher is not formally trained in listening techniques, if she develops a warm, friendly atmosphere with her pupils, she will find that learning through attentive listening will take place. Children cannot be made to listen, they must *want* to do so. Children may develop poor listening habits in a hostile classroom environment because they feel threatened either by the teacher, the group, or both of these.

It would appear that educational attitudes and processes have also contributed materially to the development of poor listeners. For years it was believed that listening depended upon the ability to hear and the child's intelligence, and that schools could do little about either of these. This would be equivalent to saying that reading ability depended only upon eyesight and intelligence. Equally erroneous was the point of view that practice and intelligence were the only significant components of efficient listening? Although most of a child's day is devoted to activities that require listening skill, there has been inadequate training in this area. Teachers and curriculum builders have assumed that because a child could *hear*, that he could automatically listen and comprehend. Obviously, it is an error to assume that listening, especially on complex levels, is something that a child does naturally. Training must go beyond teachers' well-meaning admonitions, "Now children, please pay attention," or "Please listen carefully." There must be an appreciation of some of the problems encountered in listening. For example, Wiksell[3] wrote that in reading, a child is able to adjust his speed to the degree of difficulty of the material; however, when listening, such an adjustment is not possible because the speaker sets the pace and the listener must try to follow. A spoken word is gone on the wings of sound and there is no time to retrace one's steps and reflect. Another cause of poor listening behavior may grow out of instructional procedure. Children are not challenged and stimulated by a dull rehash of textbook assignments which frequently terminate in a "ping-pong" type question and answer period. If a teacher can perform the difficult task of personalizing instruction i.e. showing children why subject matter is important to them as individuals, then the teaching of listening is simplified. Although they comprise only a fraction of the school day, periods devoted to storytelling, role playing and creative dramatics can contribute much toward the growth of good listening habits among children. The attention and response of the class in the story situation should assist an instructor to understand what contributes to good listening for the group as well as for individuals within the class.

TELLING AND LISTENING

Because so much attention is currently devoted to promoting group-mindedness among school children, it will prove helpful to examine the contribution of storytelling to acceptable group listening behavior. Those who have worked with children know that they are easily distracted by miscreants in a group. On the other hand, story interest can be so high that the group can exert considerable pressure for conformity upon a mischievous youngster. When listening is the thing to do, more children will listen! It has been found that stories which have outgrown their effectiveness for a child in the home situation because of repeated telling, have been received enthusiastically by the same child in the classroom. Group sharing of responses is indeed an important attribute in storytelling. A child may be fascinated by the reactions of others to a story which is very familiar to him.

Many factors enter into the degree of empathetic response a class registers for a story. Among these are the several items involved in choosing the right story for a particular age group, the preparation of a story, the mode of presentation and the use of visual aids. Good listening results from an interrelation of each of these factors. The following additional suggestions will assist to make telling and listening close companions. A storyteller must be sensitive to signs of poor listening as she tells her story. The shuffling of feet, whispering and yawning are overt indications that attention has strayed. More subtle signs of inattention, however, are of equal importance to a teller. The vacant stare, while not distracting to other members of a class, indicates a lack of interest. The day-dreaming child will fail to react immediately to a humorous turn in a story, although he will respond to gesticulation or radical changes in voice by the storyteller. Exaggerated laughter or surprise likewise indicates that a child is not following the story. A teacher who is constantly alert to these and other covert signs of inattention, will be a better communicator. She will want to determine why a child is not listening, and will make a special effort to accommodate this individual in her next story. For example, after school she might ask the child if he enjoyed the story. Regardless of the answer, (which would probably be in the defensive-affirmative), she might then ask him to help her choose a story for the next session.

An objective teacher will also analyze her own presentation for possible causes of inattention. It has already been stated that the proper technique for storytelling is interpretation, rather than acting. The story is chosen for its intrinsic merit and not for its potential value as an acting piece for a raconteur. Thus, throughout a presentation, the emphasis is on the story and the reactions of those who hear it. Fortunately, unlike an actress who plays before a darkened house, a storyteller interprets in a well-lighted classroom where she can see the responses of her listeners. If she adapts to the needs of her group, if she is expressive with her face and voice, the larger, overt physical gyrations of an actress are not necessary for maximum listening.

TESTING LISTENING EFFECTIVENESS

Storytellers frequently ask themselves, "How am I doing?" "Do my children respond because they love the story period or are they really absorbing ideas?" If the interest with which a group listened can be determined, improved story selection and presentation may result. Some of the means of measuring listening are as follows: Stories may be told back by the children. By asking two or three children to tell the story as they heard it, their degree of attention can be determined. For example, one child could be asked to start a story, another to tell a sequential part of it and a third child could be asked to provide the conclusion. Usually volunteers are asked to start tell-back. A child who had not volunteered may be asked to pick up the thread of the story from the first student. Another variation of tell-back consists of such questions as, "Who can tell us the names of all the characters in the story?" or "What character did you like best, Steven?" or "What was the most exciting part of the story for you, Susan?" A third form of recall is that of showing pictures from a well illustrated book and asking members of the group to reconstruct the story from the drawings. Children who fail to respond adequately during tell-back should not be reprimanded. This period following a story is merely a measure of listening. It has served as a technique to motivate a better response for the next story.

Asking each child to draw a scene or character from a story he has just heard may also serve as a measure of listening. The results of this exercise do not necessarily mean that overall comprehension of a story has taken place. Teachers have found that children will sometimes concentrate on an especially interesting incident or a situation that was vividly described. Child drawn pictures may also be used for tell-back to reinforce the story. Story acting may reveal how well a child listened. This is an especially valid measure if the role calls for both action and dialogue. This form of follow-up usually does not screen a large segment of a group because participation should be voluntary. A child who is reluctant to act may have listened attentively, may understand the story, but might suffer from stage fright. Regardless of which form of follow-up is used, a teacher should never reveal by her manner or her measure that she is testing the listening of her class. The odiousness of a test should not tarnish the joy of listening to stories.

SUMMARY

This chapter has indicated the inadequacy of listening habits of today's school children and has suggested means of improving attention during storytelling sessions. Setting the stage for good listening requires the elimination of any distractions and the creation of comfortable conditions for the listeners. Storytellers must view their efforts objectively and avoid mannerisms that detract from the story's content. Good listening is mandatory if storytelling is to promote feelings of group-relatedness, idea sharing, interest in problem solving and an appreciation of good literature. No means of measuring listening is foolproof. An inattentive child may have heard the story before, may understand a story but possess little artistic ability, or he may be fearful of self-expression. As far as listening is concerned, a storyteller's goal may be two-fold: (1) The discovery of factors of motivation which best influence her class to listen, and (2) The constant improvement of her techniques as a storyteller.

1. Gloria L. Horrwith, "Listening, A Facet of Oral Language," *Elementary English*, 43, December, 1966, pp. 858-859.
2. Ralph G. Nichols, "Teaching of Listening," *The Educational Digest*, Nov. 1949, p. 34.
3. Wesley Wiksell, "The Problem of Listening," *Quarterly Journal of Speech*, 32, December, 1946, p. 506.

8

Visual Aids

PURPOSE

The purpose of employing visual aids when storytelling is to enhance the material being presented and thereby assist in the realization of a story's objective. The use of puppets, flannel board objects, chalkboards, artifacts and pictures are justifiable to the extent that they clarify a story's content, and do not detract from it.

DETERMINANTS IN CHOOSING VISUAL AIDS

A visual aid must be appropriate to be effective. A narrator should ask herself, "Is this visual aid suitable for the mental age of my class?" Assuming that the item is appropriate in this regard, the next question might be, "Does this aid clarify the point to be stressed in my story?" *An aid must stress the point a storyteller is trying to make.* When conducting an Indian unit, one teacher ran into difficulty by displaying a totem pole made by the Haida of British Columbia when telling a story about Navaho culture. A child in the class, who had lived in Alaska, pointed out this obvious error, much to the teacher's distress. Visual aids must belong to the story and not be introduced simply because of their novelty. Choosing a visual aid may be limited to the equipment that is available. The lack of opaque and slide projectors may eliminate some stories. If a story with a flannel board is planned, the board and easel should be available at the appointed hour. If a story is to be told in a school or library other than the one normally used, the program chairman should be apprised of the storyteller's needs in advance. Similar arrangements should be made for staging and properties required for puppetry. Those who tell stories soon learn that visual aids are usually time consumers. Ample time must be provided to use them effectively.

TYPES AND USE OF VISUAL AIDS

A storyteller is the most popular and effective visual aid! In addition to the narrator, there are three forms of visual aids frequently used in storytelling. These consist of objects mentioned in a story, puppets, and flannel boards.

Objects Mentioned in the Story

When using items mentioned in a story such as Indian grinding bowls, clothing, or baskets, it is preferable to show these objects after the story has been told. More creativity on the part of the children is involved if they build a mental picture of a teepee or an animal based on the story-teller's description, *before* seeing the object. If a narrator said, "Bill's favorite sled dog was named 'Wolf'" and simultaneously displayed a picture of the animal, every child would see the same dog, and little thought would be given to the matter. However, if the dog is vividly described, each listener will develop his own mental image of Wolf and thereby participate in the story more intimately and creatively. Another advantage of showing the picture after the story is the unbroken continuity of the presentation. Delay, digressions and loss of interest due to some children's failure to pick up the thread of the story sometimes results from punctuating telling with picture showing. If the visual aids are durable, there are advantages in allowing children to handle the objects after a story has been told. It is not advisable to have the teacher explain an object and then start it on its way around the class while she continues to describe another visual aid. This practice puts one visual aid in competition with another. The preferred method is to place the items, after they have been explained, on a table and permit the youngsters to examine them at their leisure.

The use of visual aids will be more successful if a few simple suggestions are followed. All aids used should be large enough to be seen easily from the back of the room. When displayed, the item should be held high enough for all to see. Do not let lecterns, flag stands or other classroom furnishings obscure the children's sight line. If the students have faith that the storyteller will display an object long enough for all to see, better classroom decorum will result. Whenever visual aids are shown, the teacher should make certain that the audience is reminded of the relationship of the visual aid to the story they have just heard. Attention should also be directed to aspects of an item that might be lost in a casual inspection by a child. Interesting details of a wood carving, for example, should be pinpointed by the teller. By showing objects at a story's end and taking time to discuss them, the teller will learn which items are most effective to the development of a story. Lastly, the visual aid should be so familiar that it can be handled with ease and confidence. If primitive man's tools for making fire by friction are being displayed (such as the bow, spindle, socket and board) they should be assembled into position without fumbling or dropping parts of the assembly.

Puppets

The term "puppets" has been known to include everything from finger-plays to marionettes. The discussion in this text, however, will be limited to stick puppets and hand puppets because marionettes are a type of puppet which are quite complicated for children in elementary school classes to use. Although storytelling with puppets does not take the place of creative drama resulting from story-acting described in Chapter 5, it nevertheless may contribute richly to a child's development.

Values

Puppet play helps a teacher understand her class members more fully. Youngsters identify puppets with real people and actual life situations. A child who acts the part of a father in a story and who is prone to be antagonistic toward his make-believe family, might be revealing inner feelings that explain in part the puppet-operator's cause of nail-biting or other forms of emotional maladjustment. Puppet play may serve as a stepping stone to other forms of creative dramatics. Some children who are afraid to participate in story-acting, will often volunteer to take part in a puppet play. The puppet serves as a crutch, a means of detracting attention from the child to the puppet, and consequently reduces some of the pressure felt by the child when performing before other class members. Because the puppet-actor normally is not visible to the audience, puppet story-acting has proved to be an easy first-step for some youngsters toward the development of poise in oral communication. This activity not only helps a child overcome stage fright but it also encourages the development of an expressive inflectional pattern. It has been stated that the child usually is not visible during production, and facial expression cannot be forthcoming from the puppet itself. The young actor must be helped to identify fully with the part he is playing and reveal his feeling through his voice . . . through his *inflectional pattern*. Useful exercises that will assist a child to achieve inflectional flexibility may be found in the Appendix. Story-acting with puppets also helps children to adjust to and become cooperating members of a group. This process may be assisted by stressing the importance of working as

a team and not as individuals. A child who becomes petulant and refuses to let his puppet play in a story, must be made aware that the entire
casts' success is dependent upon his cooperation. A child not only experiences speech improvement and emotional and intellectual development through "putting words in a puppet's mouth" but he may also be
given an opportunity to improve his artistic ability. After a suitable story
has been told, members of the audience who wish to participate may be
encouraged to prepare puppets. It has been found that children usually
identify themselves more quickly with puppets they have constructed.
Lastly, this activity is valuable for the sheer joy it brings children. Puppet-
acting of stories encourages children to hurry to school in the morning!
Tom Smith knows that before long he will be Leo the Lion. Mary Jones is
eager to become a frightened Chicken Little. Time speeds away in this
magic land of adventure and fancy.

Characteristics of a Story for Puppet-Acting:

Most stories which are suitable for story-acting may be adapted to
puppetry. The first requisite is action. The tale must move briskly. "The
Three Billy Goats Gruff," "The Little Red Hen" and "The Gingerbread
Boy" are but three of many tales suitable for puppetry. Because the
preparation of puppets is so time-consuming, stories selected should be
those which the children will want to repeat. Generally, stories which
are in demand for retelling, as far as interest is concerned, will be safe
for puppet-acting. The story should contain characters that present
challenging, imaginative subjects for puppet construction that should
not be impossible to construct. For example, a child might be able to
sketch the fierce countenance of the North Wind but be at a loss to draw
a gnu. Showing the children a picture of a gnu for reproduction destroys
much of the creativity that should attend art work of this nature. Instead, a teacher might create a mental picture for the class by saying,
"Today, boys and girls, I am going to tell you about a strange-looking
animal that lives in far-off Africa. It is the size of a large deer and has an
ox-like head and horns. Its tail and mane look like those of a horse. It is
brown and stands four and one-half feet high. That is the distance from
the floor to this mark on the chalkboard." After the children have had
the creative fun of trying to draw a gnu, they should be shown a picture
of one. A final characteristic of a story for puppet-acting concerns its
number of characters. The size of a puppet stage usually determines
how many characters can be accommodated. Usually six children and
their puppets will prove to be the maximum number that can be handled
satisfactorily in one scene.

Producing a Puppet Story:

The requisites for a story suitable for puppetry have already been discussed. However, the children-participants should have some voice in the selection of a story. A teacher might select several stories with desirable characteristics and the students could select from these. Primary grade youngsters could vote for the tale of their choice. Middle and upper grade children should have the same privilege or, being more mature, they should be encouraged to write a story of their own. Character casting is actually preliminary to puppet-making for each actor should construct his own puppet.* Actual casting is preceded by orientation to the story explained in Chapter 5. Even though a child will not be visible to the audience when his puppet is manipulated, it is necessary that he go through the procedure of standing before his peers and characterize his puppet in some way. If he is playing the Papa Bear in "Goldilocks and The Three Bears" he might share the bear's reaction when it discovered that someone had been sleeping in his bed. This helps him to "feel" the part and influences his inflectional pattern as he speaks for his puppet. Every scene in a story should be assigned a different cast, if necessary, to insure a role for each child. In addition to developing a sympathetic identification with the parts they are to play, the actors must be made aware of the mechanics of puppetry. They should hold their puppets at the correct height during the presentation. If the puppet is held too high, the child's arm will be exposed; if the puppet is held too low, the character will appear to be walking on his knees. Either of these conditions will cause undue laughter and destroy artistic illusion. The evaluation of puppet acting will follow essentially the same lines as those set forth in Chapter 5 for story acting. Emphasis should be placed on inflection, projection of the spoken word and its intelligibility. The children should agree, beforehand, on standards for helpful conditions backstage, such as the absence of noise, correct handling of puppets, cooperation with the group and willingness to follow instructions. Praise must not be too lavish or too scant. Puppetry, like story-acting, must leave the participants feeling adequate and encouraged.

Flannel Boards

Although a told story followed by illustrations is more conducive to creative thinking by the listener than a flannel board story, the latter (like puppetry) serves an important function in storytelling.

---

*Directions for puppet and stage construction are included in the Appendix.

Values:

For years educators have appreciated the value of visual aids in the learning process. They agree that some children learn more quickly with visual aids rather than with auditory stimuli. Along with storytelling, the teaching of spelling, arithmetic, science and other subjects can be enriched and stimulated by use of flannel board stories. Like the puppetry activity, flannel board stories may be integrated with art to facilitate the child's artistic development. Once a group has decided upon a story, all members may assist the teacher in preparing the story's pictures for mounting. The children may also derive aesthetic pleasure from drawings they make for flannel board application. Flannel boards have high entertainment value and they rightfully have been referred to as magic boards. Youngsters never seem to tire of seeing pictures cling to their near-vertical surfaces. An introverted child may be encouraged to participate in group activity by placing one of the pictures mentioned in the story on the flannel board. This is certain to be a successful experience and it will encourage him to try again. Nursery and kindergarten children work tirelessly and imaginatively building on a flannel board with "blocks" of different sizes, shapes and colors. Flannel boards may be used as a means of follow-up to reinforce a story that has just been told. For example, after telling "Jack and the Beanstalk" a teacher may say, "Children, you have just heard the exciting adventures of Jack. Will you raise your hand if you would like to help us tell the story again?" There is usually an enthusiastic response at this point and the teacher will then produce the flannel board and pictures for the story which have previously been arranged in numerical order. Then she asks, "Who can tell how this story begins?" Mary volunteers, "Jack was lazy and lived in an old house with his mother." The teacher says, "Mary, you listened carefully. Would you like to put Jack's house on the magic board?" This method is continued until the children have retold the story they have just heard. They are rewarded for volunteering by being permitted to build a story with pictures. Use of a flannel board as "feedback" permits a story to be told initially with maximum imaginative play. In addition, the children are stimulated visually as the story is retold.

Procedure for Use:

Flannel boards may be constructed in any shape and size and the latter will determine in part, the procedure for use. Small lap boards are balanced against the body or held as a teacher sits before youngsters who are usually on floor mats before her. If a large, easel-type board is used, care should be taken to see that it is firmly anchored. The professional aspects of a flannel board presentation are lost when flimsy supports waver or the board crashes to the floor. Easel-mounted boards frequently are adjustable which permits kindergartners to reach and see the board with the same ease enjoyed by sixth graders. Regardless of the size board used, it must be easily seen by all members of the audience. With large boards, a teacher should stand to one side as she works, being careful not to obstruct the view for children sitting along the sides of the room. Pictures should be arranged in proper sequence before beginning a story. The order should be double-checked before beginning narration. This procedure is simplified if a number is placed on the back of each picture. The latter should be held or placed facedown, with the numbered side up. If possible, pictures should be kept out of sight before placing them on the board. Each object should be a surprise. Usually, a picture will be placed on the board simultaneously with the pronouncing of the word that identifies it. For example, "At that moment Jerry saw an Indian (teacher places picture of Indian on flannel board) emerge from the forest." This procedure may be varied. If a teacher is telling a participation story involving identification of a described picture, she might say, "It is round, red, grows on a tree and makes delicious cider. What is it?" When the children respond, she places a picture of an apple on the flannel board. Pictures must be involved in the immediate action or they detract from the story. As soon as the action sweeps past the picture of a character, even though the narrative returns to the same picture later, it should be removed from the board. For example, when retelling the story of "The Three Little Pigs," the three pigs might be shown walking down the road together on their way to build their three houses. When the story shifts to the little pig who built his house of straw, the other two pigs should be removed from the board. It is disconcerting to have pictures slide from the board before their removal is desirable. Instruction for preparation of both flannel boards and flannel board objects that will *cling* are contained in the Appendix.

SUMMARY

This chapter has stressed the importance of employing visual aids which contribute to the development of a story. Visual aids should not be introduced simply because they are novel. Visual aids most frequently used in storytelling are the objects mentioned in the story, puppets and flannel boards. When properly employed, these aids should reinforce the story in the mind of the listener and encourage creative participation.

Appendix A

Voice Improvement Exercises

EXERCISES FOR FREE SPEECH TONES

Conditions which are conducive to free speech tones are necessary before beginning voice exercises. There must be bodily relaxation and control of breathing must be achieved. Two fifteen minute drill periods daily, consistently observed, should appreciably contribute to a storyteller's mastery of delivery.

Relaxation

1. Sit comfortably and let the head move downward relaxing neck muscles. Move the head slowly from left to right until neck muscles feel relaxed.
2. Lie down and consciously relax the entire body beginning with eye closure, feel the brow, lips, lower jaw, arms, hands, fingers, legs, feet and toes relax. This drill may be conducted partially when standing or seated. Watch for opportunities to relax when waiting for traffic lights, restaurant orders, etc. . ... The more relaxation is practiced, the more instantly it may be achieved.
3. From a standing position, let the head move downward, bend at the waist, let the shoulders droop and the arms hang limply. When a sensation of full relaxation is achieved, move the torso upward, return the shoulders to an attitude of easy erectness, and finally raise the head.
4. Same as in (3) to the point where the body is bent at the waist. From this position sway from left to right as an elephant might sway its trunk. This is an excellent drill for children.
5. Counting to six in each position, move the head forward, backward, left and then to the right.

6. Let the jaw drop to an open mouth position. With the jaw down and relaxed, pull down gently on the chin and move the jaw in a circular manner to relieve muscle tension.
7. Relax and whisper "oh-ah." Now vocalize the same sounds keeping your throat and mouth as relaxed as possible.
8. Whisper "oh" and increase the whisper to vocalization. Maintain the feeling of relaxation.

Control of Breathing

1. Exhale then inhale deeply. As you expel the air, count as long as you can comfortably do so. Repeat two or three times and attempt to increase the count without losing the sensation of comfortable exhalation.
2. Inhale just enough air to count to ten comfortably. There should not be a volume of air to exhale at the termination of the count. Repeat this exercise with counts of 5, 15, 20, 25 and 30.
3. Inhale deeply and exhale counting aloud as follows: 1,2,3,4; hold, 5,6,7,8; hold, 9,10,11,12, etc. as long as exhalation is not forced.
4. Walking at a normal stride, inhale for six paces, hold for two, and then exhale for six paces. Vary the number of paces to develop facility in estimating the amount of inhalation and exhalation required.
5. Lie down, breathe normally and note that breathing is "centralized" toward the base of the rib cage where the lungs are larger than they are at the apex and the ribs are more flexible. Place your hands at the base of the rib cage and feel the expanding and contracting action.
6. Lie down, place a small book on the "V" to be felt between the ribs of the lower rib cage, and breathe normally. This will assist to "feel" where breathing activity should be centered.
7. Stand and speak to an imaginary person at 5, 10 and 15 foot distances; call to a person 25, 50 and 100 feet away. Let the pressure for projection come from the centralized breathing area ... "push" up from there.
8. Inhale just enough air to read the following lines:
   a. Halt!
   b. Halt! Who goes there?
   c. When love and skill work together, expect a masterpiece.
   d. I envy the beasts two things—their ignorance of evil to come, and their ignorance of what is said about them.
   e. Originality is simply a pair of fresh eyes.
   f. I served with General Washington in the Legislature of Virginia, before the Revolution, and, during it, with Doctor Franklin in

Congress. I never heard either of them speak ten minutes at a time, nor to any but the main point, which was to decide the question.

Quality

In the simplest terms, quality is a characteristic of tone, it is a personal subjective opinion which depends upon an individual's judgment of what sounds "good" or "bad" in vocalized tone. More specifically, changes in the strength and relationship of secondary vibrations of the vocal tones account for what is considered desirable or undesirable tone quality. The latter is also affected by such physical factors as a weak or cleft palate, adenoidal growths, inflamed vocal folds, weak breathing, etc. A normal, responsive physical organism is necessary if good quality is to be achieved. If we respond physically to mental reactions of fear, love, joy, etc. the character and strength of secondary vibrations of our vocal folds will assist to modulate the tone into desirable quality. This is a more complex restatement of the point made earlier to the effect that "impression precedes and determines expression." The following exercises should aid the development of conditions that are generally considered to be desirable:

1. All words containing sounds "m", "n" and "ng", are characterized by nasal resonance. Words without these sounds should not be nasalized. Strengthening muscles of the soft palate will assist in eliminating excessive nasality.

   a. Pronounce gah-ah, gah-ah, gah-ah several times. Develop an awareness of the soft palate as it raises to close the entrance to the nasal cavity on the "gah" sound.

   b. Same as exercise "a" with the substitution of "kuh-guh" for "gah-ah."

   c. Check for the presence of a weak soft palate closure of the entrance to the nasal cavity by placing a small purse mirror under the nostrils and saying, "This is the house that Jack built." The latter statement contains no nasal sounds and ideally, there would be no indication of warm air from the nostrils on the mirror.

2. Flatness and hardness may be caused by tensions in the throat and they may also result from a hard, cold, indifferent personality.

   a. Repeat exercises suggested for relaxation of the neck and facial area.

b. Read the following lines and identify as fully with the thought as
   possible:

> Never borrow
> Idle sorrow;
> Drop it!
> Cover it up!
> Hold your cup!
> Joy will fill it,
> Don't spill it,
> Steady, be ready,
> Good luck!
>
> Henry Van Dyke

> I want to be a Highbrow,
> With air of perfect poise,
> Who lifts a scornful eyebrow
> At all the rough world's noise;
> Oh, I could fill with glee so
> Desirable a shelf,
> A Highbrow seems to be so
> Delighted with himself.
>
> Berton Braley

> Tiger, tiger, burning bright
> In the forests of the night,
> What immortal hand or eye
> Could frame thy fearful symmetry?
>
> William Blake

> Out of the night that covers me,
>   Black as the Pit from pole to pole,
> I thank whatever gods may be
>   For my unconquerable soul.
> In the fell clutch of circumstance
>   I have not winced nor cried aloud
> Under the bludgeonings of chance
>   My head is bloody, but unbowed.
>
> Beyond this place of wrath and tears
>   Looms but the Horror of the shade,
> And yet the menace of the years
>   Finds and shall find me unafraid.
>
> It matters not how strait the gate,
>   How charged with punishments the scroll,
> I am the master of my fate:
>   I am the captain of my soul.
>
> William Ernest Henley

3. Throatiness or gravelly voice quality is frequently caused by a faulty breathing habit which fails to support tone throughout a sentence, especially on the final words or syllables. The improper use of chewing and swallowing muscles in voice production may also cause this abnormal condition. Persons who must speak frequently during their working day may develop voice fatigue due to misuse of these muscles. Instead of projecting tone from the abdominal, central breathing area, these individuals increase muscular activity in the throat which builds up tension.

   a. Review exercises suggested for centralized breathing.

   b. When reading, compel yourself to inhale at the completion of each sentence. Inhaling more breath than a sentence requires may find a reader beginning the next sentence with an inadequate breath supply. This may result in forcing air from the lungs and the development of throaty quality.

   c. Review exercises for breathing according to sentence length.

   d. Prepare adequately for all speaking engagements in order that fright induced feelings of inadequacy will not tense breathing muscles which in turn may deny a speaker proper breath support.

4. Breathiness is frequently caused by a speaker's failure to bring his vocal fold together tightly enough to prevent loss of air or by failure to adjust the folds quickly enough during sound production. Additional causes may be ill health that robs one of the energy needed to vocalize or fear that may literally leave one speechless.

   a. Voiceless consonants such as "f," "s" and also "sh," are the most wasteful of the exhaled breath stream. Practice an immediate initiation of vowel sound following the "h," for example, to guard against loss of breath. If tone production lags, breathiness will develop on the "h."

   b. Listen carefully to be certain that vocalization begins immediately following the initial consonant in the following combinations:

oh	ho	at	fat
heat	sheet	you	shoe
arm	farm	aye	fie
aim	shame	aim	hame

c. As a means of developing self-confidence and breath control simultaneously, practice the following lines after visualizing a situation which would justify such a reaction:

> Hold that line!
> Shoot the shortest sailor!
> Faith! Father has found his fiddle!
>
> Home is the sailor, home from the sea,
> And the hunter home from the hill.

d. Whisper each of the following vowels, a, e, i, o, u, and then vocalize them to develop an appreciation of the amount of breath wasted on whispering in contrast to vocalization.
e. Pronounce the following words being careful to expend as little breath as possible on voiceless consonants:
> fortune, ship, failure, sister, success, sing,
> summon, silent, full, fear, excel, theater,
> feign, sooth, freshen, hand, fire, session,
> hallow, hollow.

Strength

Varying degrees of strength or volume are required in daily oral communicative efforts. A telephone conversation calls for minimal expenditure of energy whereas hailing a taxicab may be a test of one's projective powers. Good projection depends upon controlled breathing, normal functioning of the vocal folds in order that a pure tone may be produced, proper modulation of the fundamental tone by secondary vibrations, and finally, the coordination of these several systems. More specifically, in order to project effortlessly in the classroom or on the playground, a teacher with a good voice must learn to pronounce vowels fully and with proper duration, must develop a pleasing rhythm as opposed to staccato speech and must articulate clearly in order that her message will be understood. Variation in pitch is also necessary for effective projection.
1. Pronounce the following words and exaggerate, in fully relaxed manner, the vowel sounds. *Think* of the word's meaning before producing it.

crash	happy	pain	bitter
privation	embrace	fear	fool
sniff	howl	growl	snarl
fluffy	slide	whimper	snap
implore	urge	free	enslaved
roll	low	rest	lullaby

2. Recite the alphabet stressing vowel sounds.

3. Count from one to ten stressing vowel sound. "Push up" from the central breathing area to improve projection.
4. Read the following commands to an imaginary person fifty feet distant. Project, do not simply increase loudness and tense throat and facial muscles.

   a. Close the gate!
   b. Call the police!
   c. Open in the name of the law!
   d. Your car's door is open!

5. Speak the following words and imagine that each time you do so, a listener calls, "I can't understand you!" Speak each word four times increasing the projection each time.

go	row	float
ahoy there	ah	oh
goat	goad	goal

6. Stand about thirty feet from a friend and begin to converse. Walk slowly toward each other as you do so. Now reverse the procedure and back away from each other as you converse. Increase or decrease projection as circumstances demand; avoid loudness and the development of laryngeal strain.
7. Strengthen weak tones by speaking the following words with enthusiasm. Think of a situation which would justify the word before speaking.

excellent	marvellous	safe	victory
ours	free	treasure	keys
voices	heat	food	serum

8. Interpret the following lines with freshness, with attention to vowel production, and with care to do centralized breathing:

   > Ring out, wild bells, to the wild sky,
   >   The flying cloud, the frosty light;
   >   The year is dying in the night;
   > Ring out, wild bells, and let him die.
   > Ring out the old, ring in the new, —
   >   Ring, happy bells, across the snow;
   >   The year is going, let him go;
   > Ring out the false, ring in the true.
   >   Alfred Tennyson

9. Projection is impaired by articulation that is hasty, indifferent and characterized by laziness of the lips, tongue and jaw. Use of a tape

recorder in recognition of articulation problems and in drill work will prove helpful.

a. Exaggerate the "t," "d" and "ing" in the following words:

world	first	coming	trying	discordant
white	ground	unstained	going	evade
mist	just	get	cawing	lightning

b. Avoid contracting the following combinations:

don't you	won't you	didn't you	going to
would you	could you	can't you	thought you

c. Read the following passage clearly with special thought to "t" and "d" sounds:

> Night's candles are burnt out, and jocund day
> Stands tiptoe on the misty mountain tops:
> I must be gone and live, or stay and die.
>   Shakespeare, *Romeo and Juliet*

Pitch

Pitch in speech is of two types i.e. *interval* or *step* which takes place between words and syllables and *inflection* which takes place during tone production. These two types of pitch in combination determine what is referred to as *speech melody.* Storytellers seek to develop a conversational style which requires a flexible, responsive vocal mechanism, a discriminating mind and a friendly, positive outlook on life. Monotonous speech may be of two types i.e. *plateau* and *monotony of variety.* A speaker with plateau monotony drones along without pitch change in a dull uninspired manner; monotony of variety is manifest in the "bishop's tone" or "sing-song" manner of presentation that finds the same inflectional pattern being repeated by the speaker without regard for the content of the words spoken. Changes in pitch reveal a speaker's intellectual and discriminatory abilities and attitudes. If a child is asked to count to ten it will probably rattle off the count without inflectional change. However, if this child is asked what he received for Christmas, his face would probably brighten and through inflectional change a hearer would know which gift was most cherished. This is pitch change in action!

1. Inflection is a continuous pitch change whereas interval is a definite step, a break in the utterance of sound. The following exercises pro-

vide opportunity to differentiate between these two types of pitch change and they will offer opportunity to sharpen one's use of them.

a. Using a piano or a musical instrument, strike notes randomly and attempt to duplicate them with your own voice.

b. Read the following lines with pronounced use of the interval:

> Was heard the old clock on the stair,
> "Forever—never!
> Never—forever."
>   Longfellow

c. Speak the following lines haughtily; eagerly; compassionately; angrily; sadly; happily:

> Farewell!
> It was the housemother!
> The window is open!
> Are you the custodian?
> Is my bath ready?

d. Read the following lines and accent a different word in each sentence each time you read it.

> I love you.
> Call my parents.
> The boat is sinking.
> This is my sister.

e. Have a friend read the following lines and as he does so, keep "score" on the number of intervals and inflectional changes:

> I must go down to the seas again, to the
>   vagrant gypsy life,
> To the gull's way and the whale's way
>   where the wind's like a whetted knife,
> And all I ask is a merry yarn from a
>   laughing fellow-rover,
> And quiet sleep and a sweet dream when
>   the long trick's over.
>   "Sea-Fever," John Masefield

f. Speak the pitch changes in an octave beginning on a low pitch and ending high; reverse the procedure and return to the low pitch.

g. Speak the words, "Answer the doorbell." indicating positive conviction, indifference, doubt, fear.

h. Read the following lines with a rising inflection:

> Is that you, my son?
> What is the price?
> Death, where is thy sting?
> Why worry?
> Who told the story?
> Where is the horizon line?

i. Read the following lines with a falling inflection:

I am alone.	The day is dark and dreary.
Come here.	Pull the trigger.
Eat quickly.	Blow the horn.

Appendix B

Suggestions for Puppets Preparation of and Flannel Boards

Hand Puppets: Although hand puppets may be made from sponge, clay, vegetables, balsa wood and papier mache; the two most popular items used for their construction are paper bags and socks. The following are directions for making paper bag puppets and sock puppets.

Paper Bag Puppets. Procure a paper bag which is as wide as the child's outstretched hand (Small candy sacks are excellent for this purpose). The face of the puppet may be put on with paint, crayon or embroidery. Yarn makes good hair. If desired, hats, crowns and jewelry may be added.

For these additional features, felt, sequins, old jewelry and material scraps are useful. The corners on the bottom of the folded sack should be bent back about one inch and stapled. Be certain that the corners are folded toward the center of the bottom as this will round the bottom of the sack preparatory to the formation of the head. Next, turn the sack inside out and stuff the head with soft paper. A piece of dowling (½" in diameter) should be placed in the center of the puppet's head during the stuffing operation. When the dowling is removed, a little hole remains for the child's index finger. Prior to removing the dowling, tie a string or ribbon snugly about the neck. This string holds the head and face in shape. When the head is finished, cut holes in the sides of the sack just below the neck for the thumb and middle finger (which are to be used as "arms"). Paper sleeves may be added if desired. The front of the sack may then be finished as a dress for a girl puppet or as a suit for a boy puppet.

Sock Puppets. Provide each child with a sock and have him cut off the foot. Gather the top of the sock (this will be the top of the head) and tie it securely. Next, turn the sock inside out and stuff with long fiber, soft paper, cotton, or kapok. As in the case of the sack puppet use a wood dowling to provide a hole for the index finger. Tie the neck securely and

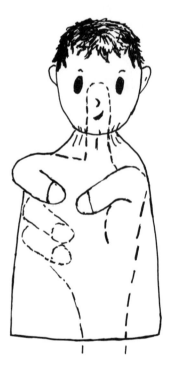

remove the dowling. The features on the face may be painted or embroidered on. If sleeves are desired, they may be fashioned from the foot of the sock and attached at the armpits (which should be cut in for the thumb and middle finger). The part of the puppet below the head may then be painted for whatever type of dress is desired for the particular puppet.

Staging. The "stage" behind which the children act, may be constructed of anything from an ample cutaway cardboard box to a large table placed on its side. One of the most satisfactory blinds for this purpose is a 4' x 8' piece of fibrous wallboard 3/8" thick. It is relatively light in weight, it allows for scenery to be thumbtacked to it, and it stores easily. The blind may be supported on the reverse side by two sawhorses. It is advisable to wire the wall board to the sawhorse to prevent the actors from being inadvertently exposed during their production! Regardless of the type stage used, it should be high enough so that the children can sit on small chairs behind it.

Construction of Flannel Boards. For the base of the flannel board you will need a piece of heavy cardboard, Celotex, plywood, Bristol board, ¼" Masonite, or the back board from carpet samples. A 3' x 4' board is recommended because this size provides space for using large pictures that may be viewed easily in the classroom. If the board is to be transported, it will prove advantageous to use either plywood or Masonite because these materials hold hinge screws satisfactorily. Boards of this type should be built of two sections, measuring 3' x 4' each. To cover the base board you will need a piece of long-fibered nap flannel (the color should be appropriate for background of stories) cut approximately 3" larger than the board. This dimension will provide a 1½" overlap on all sides. Pull the flannel tightly over the board and tack it on the reverse side. Fold it neatly at the corners and bind the edges with masking tape. If you are constructing a board in two sections, be sure to cover each section with flannel before attaching the hinges.

Procedures for Making Pictures. Pictures of people or objects (cut from magazines, coloring books, or old textbooks) should be glued or pasted to construction paper to increase their stability. When the children draw the pictures for a story, they may work directly on construction paper. Then each picture should be carefully cut out. The reverse side of the picture is then prepared for adherence to the flannel board by gluing felt or flannel on it. Some teachers prefer to use small strips of medium-grained sandpaper instead of felt or flannel.

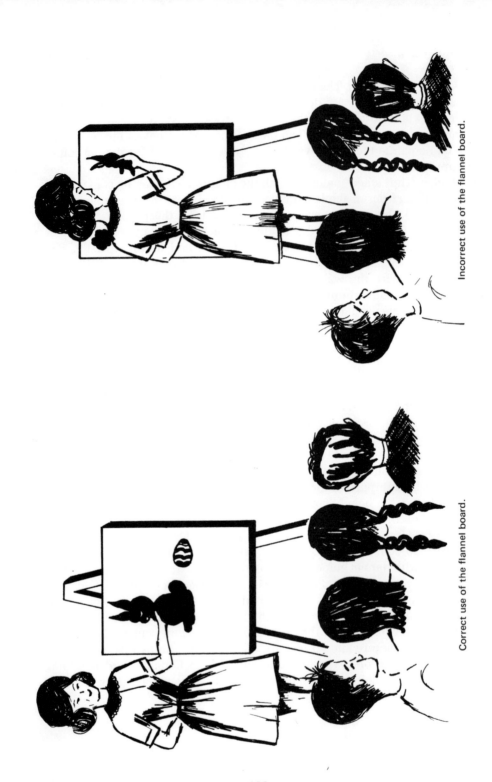

Incorrect use of the flannel board.

Correct use of the flannel board.

Appendix C

Story Index:
Author and Grade

Hume, Lotta Carswell	Favorite Children's Stories from China and Tibet	Tuttle	1962
Ickis, Marguerite	The Book of Patriotic Holidays	Dodd	1962
Keats, Ezra Jack	John Henry	Pantheon	1965
Lauber, Patricia	The Story of Numbers	Random	1961
McClung, Robert	Buzztail	William Morrow and Co.	1958
Munch, Theodore	What is Light?	Benefic	1960
Ness, Evaline	Sam, Bangs, and Moonshine	Holt	1966
Russell, Franklin	The Honeybees	Portal	1967
Sandburg, Carl	The Wedding Procession of the Rag Doll and the Broom Handle Who Was In It	Harcourt	1967
Sechrist, Elizabeth (Hough) and Woodsey, J.	It's Time for Easter	Macrae	1961
Sendak, Maurice	Higglety Pigglety Pop! Or There Must Be More to Life	Harper	1967
Smith, Emma	Emily's Voyage	Harcourt	1966
Surany, Anico	A Jungle Jumble	Putnam	1966
Tabor, John	John Tabor's Ride	Atlantic:Little	1966
Taylor, Mark	The Bold Fisherman	Golden Gate	1967
Wiese, Kurt	The Thief in the Attic	Viking	1965
Wildsmith, Brian	Mother Goose	Watts	1965
Yolen, Jane	The Emperor and the Kite	World	1967
Young, Mirian	If I Drove a Truck	Lothrup	1967
Zemach, Harve	The Speckled Hen	Holt	1966
Afanaser, Alexei	Salt	Follett	1965

4—6

Adrian, Mary	Gray Squirrel	Holiday House	1955
Alger, Leclaire	Gaelic Ghosts	Holt	1964
Ames, Gerald and Wyler, Rose	The First People in the World	Harper and Bros.	1958
Asbjornsen, Peter C. and Moe, Jorgen E.	Norwegian Folk Tales	Viking	1961
Baker, Augusta	The Golden Lynx and Other Tales	Lippincott	1960
Barker, Will	Winter-Sleeping Wildlife	Harper Bros.	1958
Bigland, Eileen	Madame Curie	Criterion Books	1957
Blackwood, Paul E.	Push and Pull	Whittlesey House	1959
Bocke, Kees	Cosmic View	John Day Co.	1958
Branley, Franklyn M.	The Moon Seems to Change	Crowell	1960
Bridges, William	Zoo Celebrities	Wm. Morrow and Co.	1959
Brown, Vinson	How to Understand Animal Talk	Little, Brown & Co.	1958

Caidin, Martin	The Winged Armada; the Story of the Strategic Air Command	Dutton	1964
Carpenter, Frances	The Elephant's Bath-tub; Wonder Tales from the Far East	Doubleday	1962
Catherall, Arthur	A Zebra Came to Drink	Dutton	1967
Cetin, Frank	Here is Your Hobby: Stamp Collecting	Putnam	1962
Chenery, Janet	The Toad Hunt	Harper	1967
Church, A. J.	The Aenid for Boys and Girls, Retold	Macmillan	1962
Cleaver, Vera & Bill	Ellen Grae	Lippincott	1967
Clymer, Eleanor	My Brother Stevie	Holt	1967
Colby, Carroll	Annapolis: Cadets, Training and Equipment	Coward-McCann	1964
Colby, Carroll	Air Force Academy	Coward-McCann	1962
Colby, Carroll	Communications: How Man Talks to Man Across Land, Sea, and Space	Coward-McCann	1964
Colby, Carroll	West Point: Cadets, Training and Equipment	Coward-McCann	1963
Colum, Padraic	The Boy Apprenticed to An Enchanter	Macmillan	1966
Compton, Grant	What Does a Veterin-arian Do?	Dodd	1964
Darling, Lois and Louis	Before and After Dinosaurs	William Morrow & Co.	1959
Edmonds, I. G.	Ooka the Wise: Tales from Old Japan	Bobbs-Merrill	1961
Ekrem, Selma	Turkish Fairy Tales	Van Nostrand	1964
Estes, Eleanor	The Hundred Dresses	Harcourt	1944
Felton, Harold W.	Sergeant O'Keefe and His Mule Balaam	Dodd	1962
Feravolo, Rocco	Wonders of Sound	Dodd	1962
Fox, Paula	A Likely Place	Macmillan	1967
Friedman, Estelle	Digging into Yesterday	G. P. Putnam's Sons	1958
Galt, Thomas F.	How the United States Works	Crowell	1965
Garner, Alan	Elidor	Walck	1967
Gottlieb, Wm. P.	Space Flight and How It Works	Doubleday	1964
Grant, Madeline P.	Louis Pasteur: Fighting Hero of Science	Whittlesay House	1959
Grimm Brothers	The Four Clever Brothers	Harcourt	1967
Hamilton, Virginia	Zeely	Macmillan	1967
Harris, Christia	Once Upon a Totem	Atheneum	1963
Hawkinson, Lucy & John	What Is A Butterfly?	Benefic Press	1958
Hawthorne, Nathaniel	The Complete Greek Stories of the Author; from the Wonder Book and Tanglewood Tales	Watts	1963

Hazeltine, Alice I.	Hero Tales from Many Lands	Gordon Laite	1961
Henry, Marguerite	All About Horses	Random	1962
Hitchcock, Patricia	The King Who Rides A Tiger and Other Folk Tales From Nepal	Parnassus	1966
Hoff, Syd	Irving and Me	Harper	1967
Holbrook, Stewart Hall	The Golden Age of Railroads	Random	1960
Holsaert, Eunice & Solbert, Ronni	Outer Space	Henry Holt & Co.	1959
Hurliman, Bettina	William Tell and His Son	Harcourt	1967
Hunt, Wolf R. and Rushmore, Helen	The Dancing Horses of Acoma (Southwest Indian)	World	1963
Hyde, Wayne	What Does a Forest Ranger Do?	Dodd	1964
Hyde, Wayne	What Does a Secret Service Agent Do?	Dodd	1962
Johnson, Gerald W.	The Supreme Court	Morrow	1962
Konigsberg, E. I.	From the Mixed-Up Files of Mrs. Basil E. Frankweiler	Atheneum	1967
Konigsberg, E. I.	Jennifer, Hecate, Macbeth, William McKinley and Me, Elizabeth	Atheneum	1967
Krumgold, Joseph	And Now Miguel	Crowell	1953
Liars, Emil E.	A Beaver's Story	Viking Press	1958
Lovett, Margaret	The Great and Terrible Quest	Holt	1967
Mann, Peggy	The Street of the Flower Boxes	Coward	1966
McGovern, Ann	Why It's a Holiday	Random	1960
Milne, Lorus & Margery	The Crab That Crawled Out of the Past	Atheneum	1965
Moody, Ralph	Wells Fargo	Houghton	1961
North, Sterling	Young Tom Edison	Houghton	1958
Olds, Elizabeth	Deep Treasure	Houghton-Mifflin	1958
Parkinson, Ethelyn	The Operation That Happened to Rupert Piper	Abingdon	1966
Picard, Barbara Leonie	Celtic Tales	Criterion	1965
Picard, Barbara Leonie	The Faun and the Woodcutter's Daughter	Criterion	1964
Pine, Tillie	The Indians Knew	Whittlesey House	1957
Porter, George	A Papa Like Everyone Else	Follett	1966
Riedman, Sarah R.	Clang! Clang! The Story of Trolleys	Rand McNally	1964
Robinson, Veronica	David in Silence	Lippincott	1966
Rollins, Charlemae	Christmas Gift	Follett	1963
Shapiro, Irwin	Heroes in American Folklore	Messner	1962

Sheppard Jones, Elizabeth	Welsh Legendary Tales	Nelson	1960
Simpson, Jacynth Hope	A Cavalcade of Witches	Walck	1967
Stirling, Nora B.	Wonders of Engineering	Doubleday	1966
Stolz, Morna	Marassa and Midnight	McGraw-Hill	1967
Tannebaum, Beulah and Stillman, Myra	Understanding Time	Whittlesey House	1958
Treece, Henry	Further Adventures of Robinson Crusoe	Criterion	1958
Updike, John and Chappell, Warren	The Magic Flute Music by Wolfgang Amadeus Mozart	Knopf	1962
Updike, John	The Ring. Music by Richard Wagner	Knopf	1964
Veglahn, Nancy	The Spider of Brooklyn Heights	Scribner	1967
Verrill, A. Hyatt	The Strange Story of Our Earth	Grossett & Dunlap	1958
Varney, Joyce	The Magic Maker	Bobbs-Merrill	1967
Wadsworth, Wallace C.	Paul Bunyan and His Great Blue Ox	Doubleday	1964
Weart, Edith Lucia	The Story of Your Blood	Coward-McCann	1960
Weisgard, Leonard	The First Farmers in the New Stone Age	Coward-McCann	1966
White, E. B.	Charlotte's Web	Harper	1952
Whitehead, Don	The FBI Story	Random House	1963
Whitney, Phyllis A.	Mystery of the Hidden Hand	Westminster	1963
Wuorio, Eva-Lis	October Treasure	Holt	1966
Wyatt, Isabel	The Golden Stag and Other Folk Tales from India	McKay	1962

7—12

Allen, Betty and Briggs, Mitchell P.	Mind Your Manners	Lippincott	1964
Andrews, Roy Chapman	Beyond Adventure	Duell	1954
Arnold-Foster, F. D.	The Madagascar Pirates	Lathrop	1957
Arnott, Kathleen	African Myths and Legends	Walck	1963
Baumann, Hans	Gold and Gods of Peru	Pantheon	1963
Beals, Carlton	John Eliot: The Man Who Loved the Indians	Messner	1957
Beebe, Burdetta Faye and Johnson, James Ralph	American Wild Horses	McKay	1964
Berganst, Erik	Space Stations	Putnam	1962
Best, Allena (Champlin)	You Have To Go Out	McKay	1964
Bixby, William	Waves; Pathways of Energy	McKay	1963
Brennan, Louis A.	The Buried Treasure of Archaeology	Random	1964
Buck, Pearl	The Big Wave	Day	1948
Chase, Mary Ellen	Sailing the Seven Seas	Houghton	1958

Commager, Henry Steele	Crusaders for Freedom (civil rights)	Doubleday	1962
Cooke, David Coxe	Flights That Made History	Putnam	1961
Crist, Eda and Richard	The Secret of Turkeyfoot Mountain	Abelard	1957
Crowther, James Gerald	Radioastronomy and Radar	Criterion	1961
Denniston, Elinore	America's Silent Investigators	Dodd	1964
Dutton, Wm. Sherman	One Thousand Years of Explosives from Wildfire to the H-Bomb	Winston	1960
Eicher, James	Law	Watts	1963
Eifert, Virginia L.	Delta Queen; The Story of a Steamboat	Dodd	1960
Epstein, Samuel and Epstein, Berry (Wm)	All About Engines and Power	Random	1962
Footman, David	The Russian Revolution	Putnam	1964
Frazier, Meta	Rawhide Johnny	Longmans	1957
Froman, Robert	Wanted: Amateur Scientists	McKay	1963
Garst, Shannon	Amelia Earhart	Messner	1947
Harris-Warren, H. B.	Dive!	Harper	1960
Harrison, C-William	Conservation, the Challenge of Reclaiming Our Plundered Land	Messner	1963
Harrison, C-William	Forest Firefighters and What They Do	Watts	1962
Hitch, Allan S. and Sorenson, Marian	Conservation and You	Van Nostrand	1964
Hodnett, Edward	So You Want To Go Into Industry	Harper	1960
Hughes, Langston	Famous Negro Heroes of America	Dodd	1958
Hyde, Margaret O.	Medicine in Action: Today and Tomorrow	Whittlesey	1964
Janson, Horst W. and Janson, Dora Jane	The Story of Painting for Young People	Abrams	1962
Johnson, Gerald W.	Communism: An American's View	Morrow	1964
Keith, Harold	Rifles for Watie	Crowell	1957
Kelly, Frank	Reporters Around the World	Little	1957
Keller, Helen	The Story of My Life	Doubleday	1954
Kennedy, John	Profiles in Courage	Harper	1956
Kjelgard, Jim	The Black Fawn	Dodd	1958
Lens, Sidney	Working Men: The Story of Labor	Putnam	1961
Lindberg, Charles	Spirit of St. Louis	Scribner	1956
McKown, Robin	Seven Famous Trials in History	Vanguard	1963
McGrady, Mike	Crime Scientists	Lippincott	1961
McNeer, May	Armed With Courage	Abingdon	1957
Paradis, Adrian	Business in Action	Messner	1962

Paradis, Adrian	Labor in Action	Messner	1963
Paust, Gilbert	How a Jet Flies	Sterling	1962
Perlman, Helen (Harris)	So You Want To Be A Social Worker	Harper	1962
Piper, Roger	The Big Dish? The Fascinating Story of Radio Telescopes	Harcourt	1963
Rogers, Frances	Painted Rock to Printed Page	Lippincott	1960
Rolfe, Douglas	Airplanes of the World 1490-1962	Simon and Schuster	1962
Ross, Frank Xavier	The World of Medicine	Lothrop	1963
Roswell, Gene	The Yogi Berra Story	Messner	1958
Scott, Jim	Bob Mathias	Prentice	1957
Scholastic Magazine	What You Should Know About Communism	McGraw-Hill	1962
Serraillier, Ian	Beowulf	Walck	1961
Silverberg, Robert	Scientists and Scoundrels A Book of Hoaxes	Crowell	1965
Stevenson, Robert Lewis	Treasure Island	Scribner	1911
Thomas, John	Leonardo Da Vinci	Criterion	1957
Turngren, Ellen	Listen, My Heart	Longmans	1956
Wacks, Theodore	Careers in Research Science	Coward-McCann	1964
Weaver, Warren	Making Our Government Work	Coward-McCann	1964
Welch, Ronald	Ferdinand Magellan	Criterion	1956
Warnecke, Heubert H.	Celebrating Christmas Around the World	Westminster	1962
Whipple, A. B.	Famous Pirates of the World	Random	1958
White, Dale	John Wesley Powell	Messner	1958
William, J. R.	Tame the Wild Stallion	Prentice	1957
Wyss, Johann	Swiss Family Robinson	Dutton	1957

Appendix D

Critique Form Suitable for Use in College-University Storytelling Classes

STORYTELLING CRITIQUE

Name:_____   Date:_____

Story: _____

	Excellent	Good	Fair	Poor
Introduction				
Was the introduction brief?				
Did the opening command attention?				
Was the conflict situation established?				
Was the transition to the body of the speech smooth?				
Body				
Were digressions avoided?				
Were key situations clear?				
Was emotional appeal used?				
Was suspense employed?				
Did the climax have emotional power:				
Did the characters seem lifelike?				
Conclusion				
Was the transition to the conclusion smooth?				
Did the conclusion draw the story together satisfactorily?				
Was the conclusion brief?				
Delivery				
Appearance: Neatly, inconspicuously dressed? Good posture?				
Gesture: Unobtrusive? Avoidance of nervous mannerisms? Appropriate?				
Language: Accurate? Colorful? Fluent? Appropriate?				
Speech: Conversational? Articulate? Easily Heard?				
Eye Contact: Furtive? Indirect? Direct? Audience adaptation during story?				
Overall Impression				

Remarks:

Index